THE LONELY LANDS

TOM ATKINSON

1·50

This is the third book in the Series

Guides To Western Scotland

First Edition 1985
Reprinted 1985
Second Edition 1986
Third Edition 1988
Revised Edition 1989
Reprinted 1990
Revised Edition 1991
New Edition 1992
Revised Edition 1993
Revised Edition 1994

Other books in this series are:-

South West Scotland, which covers the area from Dumfries to Ayr.
The Empty Lands, which covers the area from Ullapool to Cape Wrath, and from Bonar Bridge to Bettyhill.
Roads To The Isles, which covers the area west and north-west of Fort William, including the whole of Ardnamurchan, Morvern, Moidart and Morar, and then north again to Ullapool.
Highways and Byways in Mull and Iona, which covers the two most accessible islands of the Inner Hebrides.

Designed and Typeset by Luath Press, Barr, Ayrshire.

Printed and Bound by Dynevor Printing, Llandybie, Dyfed.

THE LONELY LANDS

By

TOM ATKINSON

Luath Press Ltd.
Barr, Ayrshire KA26 9TN

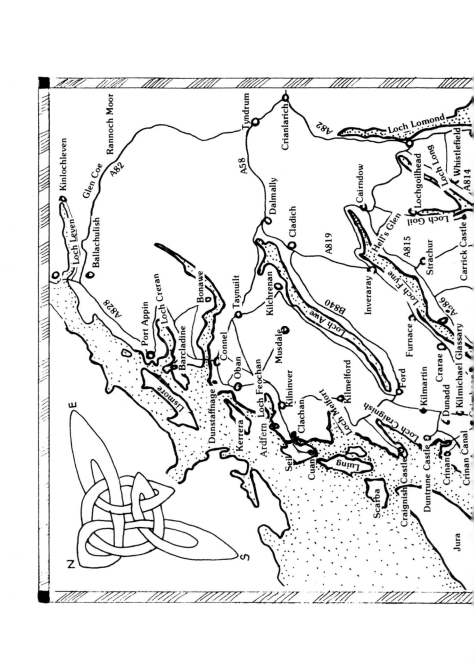

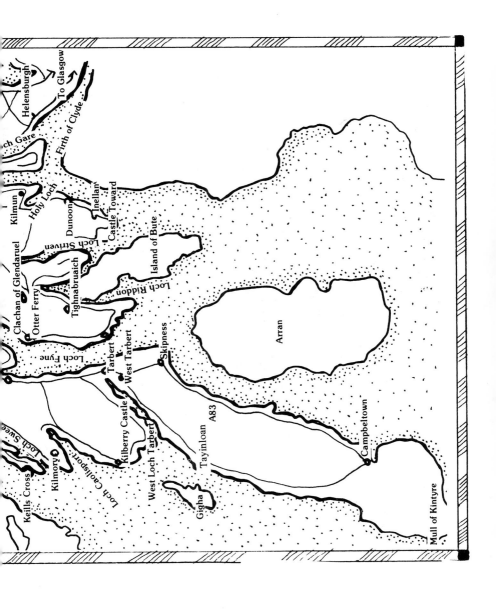

Cinntire

Gradhaich mi do mhuir 's do mhonadh,
lom do chnoc fo ghuirm an speur,
drilseach grein' air an slios taobh-gheal,
lios aosd' as milse gasda gne.

Binn guth gaoithe air do chruachan
ag eigheach air an guaillean ard;
gur riomhach do ghealchrios umad,
a' mhuir a' teannadh gu traigh.

Kintyre

I have loved your sea and moorland, the bareness of your hills under the blue of the sky, the shimmer of sun on their fair-sided flanks, old garden of sweetest and kindliest nature.

Sweet is the voice of the wind on your mountains, crying on their high shoulders; lovely your white belt about you, the sea closing in on the shore.

George Campbell Hay

Grateful thanks to the late, and much lamented, George Campbell Hay for permission, freely given to quote this part of his long poem 'Cinntire.'

CONTENTS

INTRODUCTION

The area covered by this book is vast and varied. It ranges from the outskirts of Glasgow to the remote loveliness of Kintyre, from the majesty of Glen Coe to the tiny jewelled beauty of Jura, from the busy holiday resort of Dunoon to the utter loneliness of Loch Etive, from the nuclear submarine bases on Holy Loch to Scotland's birthplace at Dunadd. Here there is choice enough, and room enough, for all.

The whole area is an ideal holiday centre, whether you seek a be-tartaned knees-up every night, or you seek the total peace of remote glens and lochs.

Most of this part of Scotland is indeed a Lonely Land. Even in these days you can find yourself a mountain side or a hill loch and spend idyllic hours in solitude. You can visit ancient places where the carved stones tell stories of centuries long past. You can wander great beaches where the Atlantic breakers roar, or where the sea is gentle in tranquillity. Indeed, it is a wonderland of beauty, surely unsurpassed in this world. And it is all available and open. The roads are good, the foot tracks mostly well-marked, the people welcoming and the hotels comfortable.

Quite certainly you need have no fears of knifing or mugging or bag-snatching. Those attributes of other holiday areas in other countries are unknown to us. Perhaps those things come with wall-to-wall high-rise hotels, and those, too, thankfully, are absent.

That is not to say that you cannot find good hotels. Far from that. Indeed, I think you can eat and drink better, in greater comfort and in more welcoming surroundings, in Scotland today than in any other place. A sweeping statement, perhaps, but I believe it to be true. So your creature comforts are assured. And should you be seeking relief for a jaded spirit, then watch the wonder of a summer sunset over Jura. Sunset comes late there but it comes bejewelled in glory, with the colours gleaming like enamel, lovely, almost unbelievable. Watching that, all the worries and fears and tensions of life are relieved.

Like all guide books, this one tries to advise you on what to do, what to see, and how to get there. However, I have tried to do much more that that. It has always seemed to me that enjoyment of any area is greatly enhanced if you have some knowledge of what has happened in the past, of what forces have shaped the countryside and the people. In this book you will find a good deal of history, a lot of description, and a fair amount of polemic, all designed to give you a better understanding of the area. Frankly, if you are the type of visitor who brings along his own cocoon, who has no interest in the past, who thinks Harry Lauder and Andy Stewart are typical Scots, then this book is not for you. But if you seek to understand what has made the things and the people amongst which you are holidaying, then perhaps this little book will help. It is written with a great love and a burning indignation. Love for a country and a people: indignation for what they have endured, and fear for a future perhaps worse than a miserable past.

The area covered in this book is virtually what was once Argyll. Properly speaking, that ancient and honourable name disappeared in the last senseless reorganisation of local government, and it mostly disappeared into the amorphous mass of Strathclyde, with its centre in Glasgow. But Argyll it remains in the mouths and minds of all those fortunate enough to live there.

The name 'Argyll' derives from Araghaidal or Ergadia, which means the boundary of the Gaels. It was at Dunadd near Crinan that, around 500 AD the first seeds were sown from which Scotland grew as a unified nation and State. The peoples who established the great network of forts around Dunadd had come over the narrow sea from Northern Ireland, and for long afterwards Argyll's links were with

Ireland, not the rest of Scotland, and that is not surprising. There are only twelve miles of sea between Argyll and Ireland, while many miles of trackless wilderness and forests divided Argyll from the rest of the country.

Yet, as the centuries passed, it was found that in fact there was easy access from the south-west to the centre and the north-east of Scotland. There was the Great Glen, there was Loch Awe and Loch Fyne, there was the narrow neck of land between the Firths of Clyde and Forth. These were means of communication, it was found, not barriers, and that communication took place, and gradually the centre of gravity of Scotland shifted from Argyll to places more central. But for centuries Argyll was the channel through which new influences travelled from Ireland to the rest of the country -- influences like the proseletysing and ascetic Celtic brand of Christianity.

The lovely island of Iona off Argyll's coast was the chief centre of the Celtic church, and for as long as that Church survived, Argyll remained at the centre of Scotland's story, although by then remote from her secular centre. Only when the Roman brand of Christianity triumphed (due largely to the efforts of Queen Margaret, the English wife of King Malcolm Canmore) at the end of the eleventh century, did Argyll become again remote from Scotland's development.

The Norsemen had for long been troublesome on these coasts and islands, and by the middle of the 12th. century they had in fact become the major influence. The Norsemen were not just the hit-and-run raiders of legend. They came, and they stayed, inter-marrying and adopting Christian beliefs. It was out of this colonisation and miscegenation that the great Lordship of the Isles arose, controlling all the western seaboard and the islands down to the Isle of Man.

The Lords of the Isles controlled great territories, and exerted great power. For reasons which we do not understand, they chose to centre that power on an insignificant island in an insignificant loch on Islay, although there they built a great stone meeting place, which is at present being excavated in a fascinating archaeological dig. In 1549, Dean Munro recorded that in the time of the Lords of the Isles, there "was great wealth and peace" in the Isles, "Through the ministration of justice."

It could not last, of course, The Scottish Crown could not accept this state within a State, and when it was strong enough to do so, it broke the power of the Lords. Although strong enough to do that, it was not strong enough in those distant parts to fill the power vacuum that resulted, and so the long years of clan feuding and warfare began.

The Lords of the Isles, were great warriors and jealous of their power. They may have occasionally recognised that their territory was part of Scotland, but mostly they held to a fierce independence, and maintained a separate fiefdom. The first Lord of the Isles was Somerled, and Argyll became the lordship of his son, Dugall. The MacDougall line held this land for generations until the Wars of Independence of the 14th. century, when, misguidedly, they opposed Robert Bruce. John MacDougall, the Lord at that time, was related to Bruce's opponents, and allied himself with the English. A sad mistake. Like everything else that stood in the way of Bruce and his vision of a free and independent Scotland, they were soundly thrashed, and lost their lands.

The Campbells of Lochawe, a comparatively minor clan, had been good allies to Bruce, and he rewarded them with grants of land taken from the MacDougalls. The Campbells prospered, and eventually almost the whole of Argyll became a virtual kingdom to them, with their head a Duke, no less. Because of this vast and unchallenged Campbell power, Argyll was spared some of the worst excesses of Highland history as rival clan chiefs drove their followers into battle after battle in an incessant search for advantage and power.

Not that Argyll was altogether insulated from history. The great dynastic and religious struggles of the mid-17th. century were as bitter here as elsewhere in Scotland, and at least twice much of

Argyll had to be repopulated by Gaelic-speaking Lowlanders from Ayrshire. The people had been killed off and the land scorched in war.

Like all things, those long years of death and destruction passed. But their passing did not bring tranquillity for the common people. The times were changing. There was a Union of England and Scotland, and the centralised Government in London was powerful: it was not prepared to allow the old Highland pattern to continue, with its constant internecine warfare and struggle for advantage.

Besides, there had been the Jacobite rebellions, centred in the Highlands, and the Crown in London rightly saw those rebellions as real threats. In particular, the 1745 uprising of Prince Charles Edward -- the Bonny Prince Charlie of song and legend -- had been close to success. The Highlands had to be tamed, and they were, in 1746 and 1747, in an episode of savagery and genocide unparalleled in its day.

The clan chiefs had been thoroughly house-broken after the 1745 rising. Indeed, their very *raison d'etre* had been removed. They were no longer needed to lead their clans into battle, and, from being Highland chiefs they turned to the pursuits of being North British gentlemen instead. For this, they required money, not men; money to build great houses, to maintain establishments in London, to gamble, whore and drink. There was money available, far more than the miserable rents that could be exacted from the peasant farmers on the clan lands. The great sheep farmers of the Lowlands and from England had money, and offered it as rent for all the vast acres of the clan lands.

Some chiefs took that road, and others hired factors skilled with sheep to work the land for them. No-one of power or authority thought to ask just whose land it was. In fact, the land had belonged to the clan, not the chief, and only legal skullduggery had vested it in the hands of the chiefs themselves.

Many of the young men had already gone from the land, encouraged and coerced into the Army and the Navy, often under the command of young scions from their own chief's family, for they too could no longer follow the traditional occupations of their forefathers. From being the military play-things of the clan chiefs -- surely the most barbarous and bloodthirsty ruling clique in all of European history -- the clansmen became the military play-things of a Government intent on spreading red blotches over the whole globe.

As the Highlanders fought and died in America, Canada, Africa and India, so their fathers and mothers, their wives and children were being systematically and ruthlessly cleared from the lands they had farmed for generations, to make way for sheep. When the chiefs were presented with the choice of money and the rich life, or continuing in the austerity of the Highlands without the old excitements of war and power, they chose the money.

It became clear immediately that the fabled clan loyalties were all upward from the clansmen to the chiefs, and did not apply in reverse, from the chief to his clan. So it was that those who legally owned the land needed more money, not men. They could get that money from sheep, but only by moving out the people, for sheep and peasant farming do not mix. And so the glens and the straths and the hills were cleared and sheep grazed where children once played. The people were moved, either to miserable little strips of land on the coast, or else to the emigrant ships waiting in the bays.

Those ships were mostly rotten hulks, unfit to venture on a duck pond, let alone the storm-tossed Atlantic, and the people were packed below in conditions that one who knew described as being unacceptable for use in the slave trade. They headed out for Canada, America, New Zealand, Australia, Africa, in a great diaspora that has left more Gaelic speakers in a Canadian province than in the whole of the Highlands.

The people were bewildered. The world was turned upside down. They had seen their cottages burned, their old folk turned out ruthlessly to die, their cattle driven off. When they protested (and it was mostly the women who protested) they were attacked by baton-wielding police and musket-wielding soldiers. Their clan chief, the father of their family (for clan means only 'family') surely could not know what was happening. So they sent pathetic messages to their chief, and he told them it was all for their own good.

And when the police and army came, and the glens were blue with smoke from burning cottages, they turned to their ministers, who told them that they were evil and sinful and predestined for Hell, and that they must recognise their duty to be obedient to the State, the kirk and their chief.

They must go, and go they did, driven like convicts to the ships, often hunted down over the moors as animals are hunted. Even those few who were left in Scotland, clinging precariously to the edges of the land, forced to take to the unfamiliar and unfriendly sea for their food, and build new paddocks from sand and sea weed, were not left alone. They, too, were an expense to the landowner or the tenant, who was taxed for the poor-rate on all those who occupied his land.

So what the potato famines did not kill, the poor-rate finished off. Most of that miserable handful was pushed off the edge, and the whole land left empty for the sheep. The Agricultural Revolution of the Highlands (and, let it not be forgotten, the Lowlands too, for it happened there also) was complete: the Improvers had triumphed and the Highlands were fruitful and profitable. *Laissez faire,* the ethics of market forces, had been given full sway, and the people perished.

It was a situation that did not last long, although vast fortunes were made while it did endure. Other countries could produce wool and mutton more cheaply than the Highlands. The descendants of those who survived those fearful voyages in the immigrant ships had their revenge. They turned out wool and mutton so fast, so good and so cheap in their new lands that the sheep industry in Scotland was virtually killed, and the sheep made way, in their turn, for deer forests, where the newly rich, tartaned and bonneted, played at shooting the stags and being Highland lairds, and the folk of the Highlands became ghillies and game-keepers and figures of fun with their pawky humour and strange ways.

Even today that is still there, to some extent, although great areas of the deer forests (which were not forests at all, but bare hillsides) now lie under conifer trees, and many of the ghillies and game-keepers run bed-and-breakfast houses or serve holiday makers in other ways.

The problems are still there, too, of depopulation, of emigration, of cultural deprivation, and there is little sign that they will be tackled in constructive ways.

But, as the Gael says, the land remains. That it is a land of emptiness is sad, but surely it is a land of aching beauty.

And yet it is *not* a wilderness. Far from being in a state of pristine, untouched nature, what we see today is all man-made. It is the result of centuries of despoliation and exploitation. The late and much lamented Frank Fraser Darling called it "a man-made desolation", stripped of its native tree-cover, over-grazed, burned and abused -- just as the native people were abused and exploited and left desolate. It is the bare bones of a land we see today, and we cannot even imagine what it used to be, with its great virgin forests and its wealth of wild life. Today even the skeletons of the mountains themselves are threatened, as plans mature to quarry the very granite for construction works in distant countries. Our forests and our fish have gone, our kelp and our coal and our oil and even our sons. Now our very mountains are threatened and are being moved to build roads and runways. It is a sad sight.

All that said, I can only express my envy for those seeing this land of wonder for the very first time, for it is indeed a land of wonder, still a delight and a revelation. Do enjoy it: do come back.

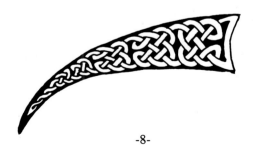

WILD CATS

LOCH LOMOND AND DUMBARTON

To many people, Loch Lomond used to mean nothing more than an hour of misery as they drove up the A82 from Glasgow to the Highlands. They may have had an occasional glimpse of the loch, and thought it pretty enough, but much of the view was that of the caravan or slow truck in front.

It is sad that this should have been so, for, without doubt, Loch Lomond, in its great basin of lovely hills, is one of the finest lochs in all of Scotland, and the views comparable with any. Today, the A82 has been vastly improved and made safer, although great care is still needed to drive it safely, and certainly the driver cannot look around and admire the views.

From Duck Bay at its broad, island-speckled southern reaches, way north to Ardlui and the entrance to Glen Falloch, Loch Lomond is a jewel, and should be lingered over. In a way, Loch Lomond, and particularly the southern part, is a great green lung for Glasgow, and undoubtedly can be very busy. You can reach Loch Lomond in half an hour from Glasgow, and many people do. But go a few hundred yards off the road, and you can be certain, even on a fine Bank Holiday Monday, of having all the quietness and peace you want.

If you must have literary confirmation of the beauties of Loch Lomond, then listen to Smollett in *Humphrey Clinker*:-

'I have seen the Lago di Garda, Albano di Vico, Bolsena and Geneva, and I prefer Loch Lomond to them all.....Everything here is romantic beyond imagination.'

It is only right when beginning a trip to the antiquities and beauties of the Highlands that one should first visit a place which has, over many centuries, played a very significant role in Scottish history. That place is Dumbarton, and it lies very close to the main A82 which runs up Loch Lomond.

To be sure, Dumbarton is not the sort of place one cares to spend much time in when on holiday, but a brisk climb up the castle rock is interesting. The view itself is fine, and somehow evocative of much of Scotland's sorry history.

Just across the river Clyde, and at the very foot of Dumbarton rock, lie the great shipyards from which the merchant navy and the Royal Navy and the ships of half the world once slid quietly. Now those yards are deserted and rusting. Up river, along the twin-highwayed 'boulevard', built as a relief measure during the economic slump of the 'thirties (and paying its way ever since), there are the houses of the well-to-do who escaped from the city, while in Dumbarton itself, clustering round the rock and in nearby Clydebank, we see housing as bad as any to be found in Scotland.

Down river, the prospect opens to far shores and distant hills, while up the once-lovely Vale of Leven there lies Loch Lomond and all the hills of the Highlands. In its effervescent growth, Dumbarton paid little attention to its long and noble history, and today almost nothing but the castle remains to remind us of a glorious past. That castle, like Edinburgh Castle, cannot confidently be dated. Almost every century, indeed generation, saw bits added and bits removed, and the result is an architectural plum-pudding of considerable attraction.

We know that Arkil of Northumbria settled there and built a stronghold in 1070, probably escaping from Norman William's 'pacification' of the north of England, which left that area a desert, but certainly the hill top, a natural strongpoint, had been fortified and inhabited many centuries before then.

Ancient legend has it that St. Patrick was born at Kilpatrick at the foot of Dumbarton rock. The legend has been questioned, but not, I think, disproved. And Kilpatrick was the western end of the Antonine Wall, erected by the Romans about 144 AD to contain the 'barbaric' Scots. Little remains of that wall today, which is not surprising, for it was built of earth and sod, and not of quarried stone like its greater brother, Hadrian's Wall, far to the south. Still, the Antonine Wall was held for about fifty years, although not without difficulty, for it was penetrated at least twice, and in the end it was abandoned when the Romans retreated to their stronger line of Hadrian's Wall, and decided that it marked the northern outpost of their empire. The 'barbaric' Scots had proved too much for them.

Dumbarton and its castle (it had many names before becoming *Dunbreaton* -- Fortress of the Britons) was the capital of the ancient Celtic Kingdom of Strathclyde, which stretched from Loch Lomond deep into Cumberland. It was a powerful kingdom, but the savage Norse raiders constantly troubled it. They attacked the castle itself in 877 and took it and ravaged the land. Only in the eleventh century did the remains of Strathclyde, with Dumbarton and its castle, become part of a unified Scottish kingdom, under Malcolm II.

Gradually added to and strengthened, Dumbarton Castle was an essential stronghold, holding down the west of Scotland, as Edinburgh did in the east. It was here that William Wallace was interned before being carried off to his barbarous execution in London after his betrayal by the traitor Monteith. The little boy-king David III sailed for France and safety from Dumbarton in 1334, and Mary, Queen of Scots, six years old and in danger, also sailed for France from Dumbarton in 1548. Dumbarton and Edinburgh Castles were the last two strongholds Queen Mary held in 1570, but so long as they were secure she still had hopes of victory. It was not to be. A very daring night raid on Dumbarton Castle on the night of April 1st 1571 was successful, and the castle fell into the hands of the Queen's enemies, and this virtually sealed her fate.

During the Civil War, the castle was in Parliamentary hands, and after the Restoration again saw battle, when the Covenanters took it, but failed to hold it, and indeed the Covenanting garrison found themselves imprisoned in the vileness of the Castle dungeons.

After the Jacobite rebellion of 1745, many Jacobite prisoners, followers of that romantic, lovely, foolish young man, Prince Charles Edward, or Bonny Prince Charlie, were held in Dumbarton on their way to trial in England. Strangely enough, although Dumbarton had been strongly anti-Jacobite, like much of the Lowlands, several prisoners managed to escape from the castle in ways that clearly indicated they had friends among the population.

The river Leven, which drains Loch Lomond and the Vale of Leven, runs by Dumbarton rock. It was once, and not so long ago, a place of immaculate beauty. Not so today. Smollett wrote a poem about it, and he makes it sound like paradise. Maybe he was prejudiced, but Pennant in 1771 supported him. 'The vale between the end of the loch and Dumbarton is unspeakably beautiful,' he wrote. Today, the new road skirts most of the detritus of dead industry, and one speeds past for the Loch shores, which retain much of their 'unspeakable beauty'.

Loch Lomond is a big loch, with the largest surface area of any loch or lake in Britain, and in parts it is very deep. At its wide lower end it is island-studded and lying in rich agricultural land. Further north, the high hills crowd forward to the very waters' edge, and there is no room there for agriculture. Suddenly, you have left the Lowlands and are deep in the Highlands.

Even today this area is not well provided with roads, and in the distant past the Loch obviously served as a route between settlements. One of the very first traces of man in Scotland is found on Inchkonaig Island in Loch Lomond, and that is a Mesolithic settlement about seven and half thousand years old. They were hunters and fishers and food-gatherers and of course left little mark on the landscape. They, and those who followed from the Stone Age to the Dark Age left many relics, though, and for those interested in those mute mementoes of long ago, Loch Lomond is very rich indeed. It is not possible here to even list the many archeological sites on Loch Lomond, but any library will provide all the information.

As the centuries passed, the area around the loch and the loch itself grew in importance. It was constituted an Earldom in the 12th cent., probably to guard the Firth of Clyde against Norse raids. That did not always work, though, for in 1263 a fleet of King Haakon's ships sailed up Loch Long, and were dragged overland from the head of Loch Long to Loch Lomond, at the place we now know as Tarbet -- *The Place of Dragging* -- and then harried the many settlements on Loch Lomond.

It must have been a fearful day when the people saw those ships sailing down this fresh water loch which had been tranquil for so long. That was in Scotland's "Golden Age", when young King Alexander was striving mightily to drive the Norsemen from the country. The Norsemen claimed sovereignty over Shetland, Orkney, the Western Isles, the Isle of Man, and Kintyre, on the mainland. In 1263, the aged king Haakon sent a large force of 20000 men and 160 ships to enforce his claims, and to destroy the upstart young Scottish King who was challenging his power.

Sixty ships, under Haakon's son and co-ruler Magnus were sent up Loch Long (the Loch of the Ships), and then dragged over land to Loch Lomond. They sailed down the loch, burning and terrorising, as was their wont, and penetrated almost as far as Stirling, hoping that the Scottish king would come forth and give battle.

Young Alexander was too wily for that. He fought a guerilla war, and a very succesful one, harrasing and picking off the Norsemen whenever he could, until their momentum was lost, and they retreated back to the sea at Largs, and there suffered a humiliating defeat at sea, a defeat which marked the end of their claims to Scotland, and allowed young King Alexander to concentrate on consolidating his country.

His death, in 1286, was tragic for his nation, marking the end of the Golden Age. He died on a night of darkness and storm, hurrying away over the Firth and along lonely paths to join his young wife Yolande. Somewhere in the darkness his horse, struggling blind, missed its footing, and the King fell to his death.

When Alexander our King was dead,
Our gold it was turned into lead.

The village of Luss, about a third of the way up Loch Lomond, is today a pretty little picture-postcard village, and busy with traffic and tourists. One hundred and eighty years ago, though, it was very different. William and Dorothy Wordsworth stayed there with Coleridge during their tour of the Highlands in 1803. Dorothy recorded that it was in Luss that they first saw houses without windows, the smoke coming out of the open spaces. The cottages were all thatched and mean, and the inn cold and unwelcoming. As a matter of fact, the Wordsworths were rather overwhelmed by the Highlands, and felt themselves totally insignificant in such grandeur after the miniature perfection of their beloved Lake District.

Another jaundiced traveller was Dr. Johnson. The day he spent on Loch Lomond side must have been wet and, to be honest, it is not quite unknown for rain to fall there. In any case, he looked out from Luss over Loch Lomond's thirty or so islands and recorded his thoughts:- '*Had Loch Lomond been in a happier climate, it would have been the boast of wealth and vanity to own one of the little spots it encloses, and to have employed upon it all the arts of embellishment.....But as it is, the islets, which court the gazer at a distance, disgust him at his approach, when he finds, instead of soft lawns and shady thickets, nothing more than uncultivated rugged-ness.*'

Well, yes, quite so. But it is the uncultivated ruggedness that makes the whole scene so very wonderful.

Looking from Luss, the nearest island in the loch is Inchkonaig, and that island was planted with yew trees on the orders of King Robert Bruce, to provide bows for his archers. It is not clear why he chose that particular place for the trees, but, knowing Robert Bruce, one can be sure that he had a very good reason for it.

Just by Inverbeg, just north again from Luss, after travelling up the now vastly 'improved' road, once so narrow and squeezed between the Loch and the hillside, a minor road to the left takes off steeply to Glen Douglas. This is a very pleasant side-trip, and if you take that road, driving carefully, to its end on Long Long, then turn right and keep right, you come to Tarbet, back on Loch Lomond.

You might well be shocked, after a few miles of that lonely wilderness, to find yourself running alongside an enormous Ministry of Defence area, with high wired fences and insignificant concrete-capped caverns dug into the hillside. You will understand what sort of loathsomeness is stored in those caverns when you drop down to Loch Long, and see the nuclear submarines there.

A footpath goes up the hill from Inverbeg, and climbs steeply through the trees, up 600 feet to the open hillside and the Fairy Loch, where legend insists that the elves and fairies come to wash their clothes. It is a pretty place, and the water is a delicate green from the dye that the elves use, for, as we all know, they are invariably dressed in green.

Ben Lomond -- *The Hill of the Beacon* -- stands foursquare

opposite Tarbet, although its vastness has dominated the view over the Loch for some miles. Probably by this time the thoughts of everyone travelling up Loch Lomond have turned to one of Scotland's most famous songs. These are the 'bonny, bonny banks' of the song. Not everyone, though, knows the origin of that song. It isn't just a love song, nor another of the Scots' nostalgic longings for home. The song, in fact, was written after the 1745 rebellion, and it tells of two Scots imprisoned in Carlisle Castle. One was to be executed and the other to be released the next day. He who was to die would take the low road -- the road of the spirit -- to his beloved homeland: he who was to be released would take the high road, but his comrade, in spirit at least, would be there first.

From Tarbet the road north, still A82, continues along the lochside. Gradually the Loch narrows, with the great heights squeezing closer, so that sometimes one can hardly realise there is a way ahead. Then, quite suddenly, on a little flat plain between the hills, the loch ends, by Ardlui, and you enter Glen Falloch with its tumultuous river. But before going further, stop and look back down Loch Lomond before leaving it behind. Some thoughtful person has arranged a car park and a convenient viewing site there. The view is quite simply splendid. You can see for miles down the narrow part of the loch, through the great gash in the surrounding mountains which tower in glory wherever you look. The colours, especially in sunlight, are extraordinary, almost unbelievable in their enamelled purity.

Loch Lomond might be a tourist cliché, the place one must travel through to get somewhere else. If you just regard it in that way, and don't stop to relish its wonders, then you will have missed something that is the very essence of the Highlands.

So far, we have been only on the busy west side of the loch, looking with appreciation across to the east. No road runs the length of the east side, but one does run about half way along, to Rowardennan.

To reach it, follow A811, signposted Stirling, from the foot of the loch at Alexandria. At Drymen, leave the main road and turn left on to B837. This is a gentle and quiet road, at least compared with A82 on the other side. If anything, the views over Loch Lomond from the east are better than from the west, and certainly the driver has more opportunity to enjoy them.

The road ends at Rowardennan, and you must (it is no hardship) return the way you came. But Rowardennan is right at the foot of Ben Lomond, and a track from there leads to the summit.

That is no Sunday afternoon stroll, though. Do not even attempt it if you are not fit and properly equipped. If there are walkers and a driver in your party for Rowardennan, let the walkers take the Ben Lomond track, but instead of bearing left up the Ben, carry straight on through wild and lovely country to Loch Ard. The driver can take the vehicle back to Drymen, then carry on the Stirling road (A84) to Aberfoyle, then turn left on B829 to the end of Loch Ard and pick up the walkers there. That would be an excellent day out for both walkers and driver.

Although it is really outside the scope of this present book, it is a superlative drive from Aberfoyle along Loch Ard to the shores of Loch Katrine. You can take a side road there -- a miniscule road off a minor road!-- running left down to Loch Lomond at Inversnaid. You have to go back the same way, then continue round Loch Katrine with its memories of Walter Scott's *The Lady Of The Lake*, through the Strath of Gartney and back to Aberfoyle. Much of that country is in the Queen Elizabeth Forest Park, and it is lovely.

There are the ruins of a fort at Inversnaid. It was built by a determined Government to hold down the turbulent MacGregors, for this was their country. It can't have been a great success, for it was burned down three times by the MacGregors.

Over a hundred years ago, Inversnaid was the inspiration for what is surely one of the most evocative poems in the English language. Gerald Manley Hopkins, then a priest in Glasgow, snatched a short holiday at Loch Lomond, and there wrote *Inversnaid.*

What would the world be, once bereft
of wet and of wildness? Let them be left
O let them be left, wildness and wet:
Long live the weeds and the wilderness yet.......

That sentiment, so beautifully expressed, well echoes the inner thoughts of every hill gangrel of today, when the wet and the wildness are threatened as never before. Even the Inversnaid burn, which inspired the poem, is but a pale shadow of what he saw, having been utilised for a (very necessary) water supply for Glasgow.

For the real walker, the West Highland Way runs up almost the full length of the east side of Loch Lomond. Even for those who are not prepared for the full rigours of the West Highland Way, it is perfectly possible, and very enjoyable, to start walking at the end of the road at Rowardennan, enjoy the track from there to the head of Loch Lomond (the track keeps close to the Loch all the way, and there are no steep hills to negotiate) and then rejoin the main road at Ardlui, where again transport can be waiting.

Of course, if you are going north to the Highlands from Glasgow, there is a perfectly good alternative to the road up Loch Lomond, and this is to follow the A814 past Dumbarton and Helensburgh, up Gare Loch and Loch Long, and join the Loch Lomond road at Tarbet. Although surely not as scenic as the Loch Lomond road, it has its own attractions and avoids a lot of traffic congestion.

Helensburgh, the first town to be passed on the A814, is a rather strange place, which seems to suffer from an inbuilt schizophrenia. It is very close to Glasgow, of course, close enough to be reached on a day out. So it offers all the joys of a seaside resort, and they are many. Up the hill, though, are the fine large houses of those who have sought Helensburgh as their ideal residence, commuting daily to Glasgow.

The town itself, when it became a burgh in 1802, was laid out in deliberate imitation of Edinburgh's New Town. It is in a fine position, looking out over the Firth of Clyde and Gare Loch. The town was first established in 1774 by Sir James Colquhoun of Rossdhu on Loch Lomondside. He named the site after his wife, and it soon became popular for the new craze of sea bathing -- not bathing for pleasure, of course, but for its supposed therapeutic effect. In 1812, the bathing-master at Helensburgh was one James Bell, and he had the brilliant idea of building a little steamboat to carry his bathers from the city to Helensburgh. That steamboat was the *Comet*, and was the first example of steam navigation in Europe. Henry Bell received the gratitude of the Helensburgh citizens for his ingenuity, and they made him Provost of the town, and also erected a granite obelisk to his memory on the town esplanade. Within a generation of Henry Bell's startling innovation, no less than fifty paddle steamers were working on the Clyde.

The railway followed, and the town grew. But it grew in a controlled and pleasant way, with broad, tree-lined streets. In 1902 Walter Blackie of Glasgow, a considerable publisher, decided to move there, and he employed Charles Rennie Mackintosh to design a new house for him.

Walter Blackie was just a little careful with his money, and Mackintosh did not have the free hand he would have liked to execute his 'total design', which included every part of the house and its fittings even down to the cutlery. But Hill House is a magnificent example of the Mackintosh interpretation of *art nouveau*. You can see it today in Helensburgh, for it is now owned by the National Trust for Scotland, and has been carefully renovated.

It was in Glen Fruin, just south of Garelochhead, that the MacGregors finally stepped over the barriers of the permissible, and as a result were outlawed.

The MacGregors were a particularly troublesome lot, even for those days in the early 17th cent., and there had been a long-standing feud with the Colquhouns. It is said that the feud began a century earlier, when the Colquhouns refused food and shelter to two benighted MacGregors, who at once took and ate a Colquhoun sheep.

They were hanged for that. In the complex pattern of clan custom it might be that the Colquhouns were thus responsible for the subsequent enmity between the two. Be that as it may, the MacGregors were without question unruly neighbours.

At Glen Fruin, the Glen of Sorrow, one winter's day in 1603, the Colquhouns allowed themselves to be ambushed by two forces of MacGregors, and over a hundred Colquhoun men were killed. Worse than that, it was alleged that the MacGregors slaughtered a party of thirty students from Dumbarton who had followed the Colquhouns to watch whatever battle they might find. The MacGregors, drunk with victory, plunged into the Colquhoun lands, plundering and pillaging. It was all too much for the Government. After all, this had taken place almost in sight of Dumbarton Castle, and the Government was intent on making the Lowlands secure and peaceful.

The chief of the Colquhouns, with a sure touch of the dramatic, appeared before King James at Stirling, accompanied by the black-clad widows, all bearing the bloodied shirts of their dead husbands. Instantly the King proscribed the MacGregors. Even to bear the name was to mean death, and the King entrusted the extirpation of the Clan to the Earl of Argyll. And that in itself was ironical, for the Earl had been quarrelling with the Colquhouns of Luss, and had been actively encouraging the MacGregors in their depradations. That proscription of the MacGregors, and the right to shoot them down like dogs, lasted until 1795.

There is one sublime view along this road. Stop at the top of the hill at Whistlefield, and look across Loch Long up the length of Loch Goil. This is a twisting fiord of a loch, hemmed in by mountains, and narrow. It is not easy to find a good view of it, especially when travelling along its length. That view from Whistlefield is grand and dramatic, and alone would make this trip up Loch Long very worthwhile.

Travelling this road, you are of course going past great depots and encampments all connected with nuclear submarines and warfare. You perhaps cannot avoid seeing them, but you can keep

your eyes across the Loch and enjoy views of what is sarcastically
called Argyll's Bowling Green. That is the great mass of roadless
and uninhabited hills running almost the full length of the west side
of Long Long. It is a narrow and deep Loch, sometimes
inexpressibly sad in the gloaming of a winter's day, but glowing
vibrant with colour in sunshine. Best of all, see it when the hills are
snow covered and the water blue and the roads empty.

SHAGS & GREY SEALS

RAZORBILLS & GUILLEMOTS

-24-

LOCH LOMOND TO GLENCOE & BALLACHULISH

From the head of Loch Lomond, the A82 climbs up through Glen Falloch on its way north. It is a grand road, much 'improved' these days, that follows the river before climbing out on to open moorland and finally dropping down to Crianlarich. In part, it runs through scrub forest, oak and hazel mostly, that is one of the last poor remnants of the great Caledonian Forest that once clothed Scotland and held the thin soil onto the hills, where bare rock now gleams.

Most of those forests, including that in all of this area, were felled to feed the primitive iron furnaces set up two and a half centuries ago. There were about one hundred of them altogether throughout Scotland, established mostly after the 1745 uprising, when the clan lands were opened to exploitation and depredation. It did not take long, of course, to clear off the forests, and then the furnaces closed, leaving the workers bewildered, homeless and hungry, many of them with no option but to go south to the dark satanic mills or overseas. It is an old and recurring story in Scotland. A brief and ruthless exploitation of what little natural wealth there was, then some, mostly non-Scots, escape with great wealth and the rest return to a land so much the poorer. Wood, kelp, coal, beef, and now oil?

At Crianlarich, the A82 is joined by the A85 from Edinburgh, and the two together, still the A82, head north-west towards Tyndrum and the vastness of Rannoch and Glen Coe.

Just short of Tyndrum, on the left is Dalrigh, the King's field, where King Robert Bruce was waylaid and lost the brooch from his cloak. That was the famous Lorne Brooch.

This happened in 1306, when the King, after the defeat by the English at Methvin, had retreated to the fastnesses of the High lands, where his allies were strong. He was travelling west through Perthshire to Argyll, to join with the forces of his friend Campbell of Loch Awe. At Strathfillan, MacDougall territory, his small band was attacked by the MacDougalls and routed. The King and his men scattered, and Bruce himself went south, only to be ambushed by three MacDougall men, who lived hardly long enough to regret their temerity, for Bruce was a mighty fighter for whom the odds of three to one were hardly equal. He killed all three, but the brooch from his cloak was left grasped by the hand of a severed arm from a dying man. That brooch is today in the MacDougall mansion house at Dunollie near Oban.

To the right of the road, as it runs through Strath Fillen between Crianlarich and Tyndrum, is the great empty wilderness of Breadalbane. Empty enough and wilderness enough today, but once it was populated and produced large quantities of beef. But the people

have gone, long ago, dispersed in grief to the far corners of an Empire now itself vanished. And gradually the once fertile valleys and hills are being cloaked by the rigid lines of conifers, never again to know homes and hearths and schools.

Just beyond Tyndrum the road divides. A85 goes off to the left for Oban, and A82 carries on, up the hillside and opening out to all the wildness and beauty of Rannoch and Glen Coe. It is a lovely country, breathtaking and splendid and unique. Whenever one travels that road, and however often, it never palls. Surely no other road in Britain offers so much to the traveller. It is a lonely land, and sometimes a frightening one, but never dull.

The road itself is splendid and one can drive fast if need be. It was built in 1935, with great difficulty, and replaced the old road whose remains can be seen here and there. That old road is now the long distance West Highland Way, and a fine tramp it is.

As a foretaste of the delights to come, the great shapely cone of Beinn Odhair rears up a few miles north of Tyndrum. It is a splendid mountain, soaring to almost three thousand feet from the valley floor.

Its neighbour, Beinn Dorain, is even higher, reaching almost three and a half thousand feet. Not far away, on the west side of Loch Talla, Duncan Ban MacIntyre, that astonishing Gaelic poet, lived, and he loved Beinn Dorain and composed a fine poem about it.

No mountain may compare with Ben Dorain,
a bold lofty peak, skyward yearning,
downward sweep of moor, haunt of tim'rous deer...

Like much else that Duncan Ban composed, it is a remarkable exercise, being comparable to a pibroch, with a ground first being laid, and then various changes being wrought on the basic theme. You can't say that Duncan Ban 'wrote' his poems, for he was illiterate in the sense that he had no reading or writing, but he was indeed highly literate in an older sense, the sense of the old bards, for he carried many thousands of lines in his head, and later was able to dictate his poems, and saw them in print, when they were as highly regarded as the works of Burns or Ossian.

The railway from Glasgow to Fort William and Mallaig skirts both those lovely mountains, and a dramatic section of a memorable journey that is.

By now, you are travelling over Rannoch Moor, another vast and lonely wilderness. It is a strange place, sometimes frightening, and at other times bright and welcoming, but never boring. Once, it was forested, but the trees have long gone, although great trunks and roots still lie everywhere buried in the peat and preserved there.

The very names seem to speak of loneliness -- Black Mount, Loch Ba, Carn nam Bocan (The Cairn of Ghosts), even Rannoch Moor itself.

And yet this is the fabled *Road To The Isles* of the song. On a fine spring day, with the colours bright and new, the lochans sparkling and the birds full-throated, you can well appreciate the liveliness of that song.

Kingshouse Inn is off to the right, on the old road. This was an old droving inn, and a place of shelter for travellers and soldiers. Those drovers of old were hardy characters, and they needed to be. Apart from the hardships of the road, they had to defend the herds of cattle, and protect the large sums of money they carried. That can't have been easy when they had to pass through country inhabited by people who were almost professional cattle thieves. They were armed of course, those drovers, and very ready to use their arms. Indeed, even during the years after the 1745 rising when arms were prohibited in the Highlands, the drovers were exempted from that law.

It was at Kingshouse that Colonel Hamilton was billeted, with a large number of men, and with orders to exterminate any who escaped from the massacre in Glencoe. He arrived too late for that, and those who had escaped from that fearful dawn were scattered in the hills and passes, but he and his men drove off all the cattle and burned and looted the houses.

Just by Kingshouse, on the opposite side of the road, a ski lift

GLENCOE

can take you high into the remote mountains. It was the first ski lift in Scotland, and, very wisely, runs throughout the summer when there is no snow for skiing, but the views are awe-inspiring. You can travel effortlessly and delightfully to heights it would take a good walker all day to reach, and then stroll amongst the glory of those high places.

Glencoe -- The Glen of Weeping -- will forever be associated with the events of that winter dawn in 1692 when the people of the Glen woke to find that their guests were barbarously slaughtering those whose fires they had shared and whose bread they had broken. Of all the beastliness which is smeared over Scotland's blood-boltered history, nothing has left such scars -- indeed, open wounds -- as this particular episode. It isn't as though it was an especially big massacre by the Highland standards of the day -- only thirty eight people were killed, although many more perished in trying to escape over the hills. It isn't the fact that it was done in cold blood and not in the heat of battle -- the massacre at Dunoon (also carried out by Campbells) was equally cold-blooded, but only historians speak of that today, while the killings at Glencoe are known to all, and will never be forgotten.

What made the Massacre of Glencoe so special and so horrible was that it was done in violation of age-old custom, the custom of hospitality. It was the treachery, not the killings, that made it unbearable. It all happened in this way.

King Charles II died in 1685, and was succeeded by his brother James, who promptly became a Roman Catholic, like his dead brother. This was not to the liking of the English, and there was great unrest, so much in fact that the King, who had never shown much enthusiasm for the job anyway, left the country in 1688, and was held to have abdicated. The Parliament invited his daughter Mary, a Protestant, and her Dutch husband, William of Orange, to take the throne. This particular piece of Parliamentary chicanery has become known as The Glorious Revolution.

There was little opposition to the move in England, nor indeed in the Lowlands of Scotland, but it was very different in the Highlands, where the old Catholic religion still ruled, and where loyalty to the Stewart line was strong. There was a rising, and an English army was annihilated by the Highlanders at the Battle of Killiecrankie, just north of Pitlochry. But the Highland leader, Claverhouse, was killed, and the rising soon ended. The Highland chiefs who had joined the rising were offered a pardon if they swore allegiance to William before January 1st, 1692. With much heartsearching and after much discussion, they agreed, and all but one, MacIan of Glencoe, took the oath in time.

This was much to the chagrin of the Government and its Scottish allies, who had been hoping for an excuse to break up, if not positively extirpate, the Highland clans. It was in the Highlands that a great deal of opposition still remained to that Union of the Crowns of England and Scotland which had brought the Stewart line to the throne of England, but which had resulted in Scotland losing the national independence of centuries.

MacIan, of the MacDonald Clan, was an elderly man, and a stubborn one, and it was not easy to persuade him, but it was finally done, and in the depths of winter he left his home in Glen Coe for Fort William, to take the oath. But there was no one there empowered to do that, or so he was told. MacIan had to travel to Inverarary, and a vicious journey that was through the snow-stacked mountains. He arrived there on January 2nd, but the Sheriff was not there. He did not return until January 5th, and then recorded MacIan's submission.

It was too late: the authorities had the chance to eliminate at least one of the troublesome clans, even if their hopes to deal with the rest were ruined. It was the King himself who signed the order to annihilate the MacIan's, but those who engineered it, organised it and carried it out were Scots.

In February 1692, Campbell of Glenlyon moved into Glencoe with his troops and billetted them in the houses, two weeks before the day set for the killings. They said that there was no accomodation for them at Fort William. There must have been some bitter thoughts amongst the MacIans at this, for it was the Campbells who had dispossessed them of their hereditary lands in Ardnamurchan not so many generations ago. Glenlyon's orders were clear. He was to secure all avenues *'so that the old fox nor none of his cubs, may get away. The orders are that none be spared, to 70, of the sword, nor the Government troubled with prisoners.'* It should have been easy, and indeed it was, but in fact many escaped, and only thirty eight died. The rest, alerted by the screams and commotion, escaped into the bleakness of that dawn and the bone-shattering cold of the hills, where many perished.

It was a black deed, done by the blackhearted. The chief amongst them, apart from the King, was the Master of Stair, who had some reason to believe that his own position of trust was not secure, and thought that this inhumanity would prove his loyalty, and also intimidate the Highlanders who, like his King, he regarded as savages.

No-one who knows anything of the story can pass through that lovely Glen without sensing something of the horrors of that dark winter dawn almost three hundred years ago. And lovely it is.

Great peaks rise sheer from the valley floor. Bidean nam Beann is there, towering 3760 feet, the highest peak in all of Argyll. At the head of the Glen, Buachaille Etive Mor, the *Big Herdsman of Etive*, soars to 3345 feet. Through a dark gorge, the river Coe enters the Glen and rushes swiftly down to the level floor and then more softly to Loch Leven.

It was in Glencoe that the Fingalians of myth and legend hunted the red deer. Up on the stark side of Aonach Dubh is Ossian's Cave, and near the foot of the Glen is the shapely Sgurr na Feinne, the Fingalian's Hill.

A number of side glens run down into Glencoe. Today, these, like Glencoe itself, are empty and barren, but when the MacIans lived there, all this land was tended. Even the hillsides were terraced to hold back the soil in the winter floods. When the soldiers left

Glencoe after the massacre, they took with them 900 cows, 200 horses and a great many sheep and goats. That is a measure of how rich this, and many other glens, once were, and could be again.

The West Highland Way, that grand foot track, does not really go through Glencoe, but takes off to the right, over a rough track, once a military road, known as The Devil's Staircase, to Kinlochleven. It was that track that was followed by so many men as they travelled to Kinlochleven to work on the great aluminium plant there, and on the dam to power the hydro-electric plant which powers the furnaces. They did not all reach the safety of their camp at Kinlochleven, or of Kingshouse: many died there in the cold and snow of the winter, and some nameless bodies were found when the spring thaws came. It was hard and vicious work, but out of it the writer Pat MacGill fashioned a great book, in which MacGill (who had himself worked as a navvy on that job) tells the story of Moleskin Joe, and of the hardships of those travelling navvies who provided the muscle power to build the great works from which so much wealth has flowed. It is unusual to find books written with great knowledge about the life of working people: Pat MacGill makes poetry and tragedy from it all.

Kinlochleven is not, of course, on the direct road north, or to Oban. It is a side track, but one that more than repays the forty minutes or so that it takes. Until a few years ago, a ferry crossed Loch Leven where the new bridge now stands, and that ferry was a frustrating bottleneck. If there were more than half a dozen cars ahead of you in the ferry queue, it was quicker to drive round by Kinlochleven. Today, with the bridge, that reason for going there has vanished, and the only reason remaining is that the road is very fine indeed. It is described as The Scenic Route, and indeed it is all that.

The road stays high above the loch for much of the way and affords intriguing views up and down the length of the island-studded water. This road was built by the labour of prisoners-of-war in 1914-18, and the road engineer must have had a touch of genius. It skirts the Pap of Glencoe and gives spectacular views of the Mamore

Forest. This circuit of Loch Leven is so much worth while that you should take it, even if your destination is south towards Oban, and it means you must cross back over the neck of the Loch by the new bridge.

BALLACHULISH AND ONICH

Although today little more than a village passed through on the way north from Glasgow to Fort William, Ballachulish was once a household name. In the 19th cent., about 17 million slates were taken every year from the huge quarries there, and exported all over Britain and to many other countries. There is a very interesting exhibition about the slate mining days in the Information Centre.

The village itself is the object of a great clear-up operation to remove the industrial detritus left from the old days. It seems to be successful enough, and presumably the raw scars from the clean-up will themselves eventually heal. The Highlands are infinitely forgiving.

Just by the hotel, which is through the village and under the shadow of the new bridge across Loch Leven, there is a wooded hillock on which James of the Glens was hanged for the Appin Murder. A monument on the top carries the inscription *In Memory of James Stewart of Acharn, who was executed on this spot on 8th November 1752, for a crime of which he was not guilty.* The story of this murder is told later, in the section on Appin, but it was here that the execution was carried out, and the body left to rot in chains.

That was not the end of it, though, for later, much later, when only wired-together bones were left to swing in the wind, the bones were taken one night, when the sentry guarding them was enticed into a nearby ale-house, and were given decent burial. One of those responsible for that was an ancestor of David Livingstone, that great African explorer, and he had to flee from Appin as a result.

The road north from Ballachulish runs by the side of Loch Linnhe through the village of Onich and on to Fort William. The

views across the loch are very fine, taking in all the great hills of Ardgour and Conaglen. Just beyond Onich a great standing stone, Clach a Charra, seven feet high, still looms at the water's edge.

CAPITAL 'E' FROM THE BOOK OF KELLS

FOXES AND BUZZARDS

APPIN AND LISMORE

When going north on A85 from Oban towards Fort William, after Benderloch and going round the head of Loch Creran, there is the Strath of Appin, and Appin itself. A strange land, rich and fertile, but somehow a very secretive land, a land that does not give itself easily and yet is very much worth the courting.

Everyone who has read Stevenson's *Kidnapped* knows about Appin, for the novel is a barely fictionalised account of what actually took place. But what *really* took place remains a mystery to this day.

The story is stark enough in its outline. It was just one more of the many effects of the genocidal policy followed by the English Crown and its Scottish jackals after the defeat of the rising in 1745. The Appin lands of Stewart of Ardsheal were confiscated and one Colin Campbell -- Stevenson's Red Fox -- appointed factor. One day in 1752 Colin Campbell was on his way through Appin to evict some tenants when he was shot from behind by some unrecognised man. Suspicion fell on Alan Breck Stewart, who fled to France with money supplied by James Stewart. James was arrested and charged with being 'art and part' of the murder.

He was tried in Inveraray, Campbell capital, by a Campbell judge and a Campbell jury. To the surprise of no-one, he was adjudged guilty, and hanged at Ballachulish.

That was not quite the end of the affair, though. Part of the sentence had been that Stewart's body was to be kept permanently on the gallows as a reminder and warning to others. Some years later only the bones were left, and they were wired together. One night the remains were taken from the gallows (stolen, rather), by a group of men who had enticed the sentry into the nearby ale house. The bones were given decent burial by three brothers, one of whom was the grandfather of David Livingstone, he of Africa.

Legend has it that the name of the man who fired the fatal shot was widely known in Appin, that it was not James Stewart, and that this name has been passed down from generation to generation of young men there.

Of course, Appin is something very much more than legends such as those of the Appin Murder. The name 'Appin', incidentally, derives from *Abthaine*, meaning the Abbatial Lands -- in this case, lands of the Celtic Church on Lismore.

From the south, from Oban, you enter Appin after rounding Loch Creran, and as you do so, you will no doubt wonder why the road goes right round the loch instead of crossing its mouth over the existing, but now disused, railway bridge. The mouth of Loch Etive, close to Oban, is crossed on such a bridge: why not Loch Creran? However, the trip round the loch is interesting and pretty enough, and the great mountains to the east are those of Glencoe. There are passes through the hills to both Glencoe and Glen Etive. They are not for the summer-time stroller, though.

There are some good walks, however, starting from the Loch. One, beginnning about a mile and half from the railway bridge, leads up to the waterfall of Eas na Circe, high up on Meall Garbh. It is a bit rough, but well worth while. There are others, not so rough, also beginning at the loch side.

Just at the bridge over the river Ure at the head of the loch, a minor road strikes right up Glen Creran. The road is a dead end, petering out after three miles or so into forest tracks, but it is a very worthwhile excursion. A track runs from the end of the road as far as Ballachulish, and that would make a fine walk for a summer's day. The glen is a grand Highland valley, sheltering beneath high hills, narrow and heavily wooded. The delightful little Loch Baile Mhich Chailean stands where the glen divides, with the river Ure running gently along the right hand part. Fasnaclaich House, where Alan Breck Stewart stayed before the murder of the Red Fox, is on the shore of the loch, and the Red Fox himself, Colin Campbell, lived in the big house where the glen divides. The road, or track, rather, continues up the left hand fork of the glen, but peters out at Elleric. It is a pleasant drive, and a better walk, with the river below and the high hills ahead. You must, of course, return the way you came, if you are on wheels, at least, and it is very much worth stopping at Glasdrun, where the main road is rejoined, to visit the Nature Conservancy Reserve there.

Back on the main road, you come then to the Strath of Appin, and although the road through this wide and fertile valley is pleasant you might well prefer to turn left on to the minor roads which follow the shore of Loch Creran to Port Appin.

The shore is deeply indented with very attractive bays -- superb for beach-combing -- and most striking views across the Lynn of Lorne to the island of Lismore.

From Port Appin there is a ferry (not a car ferry) to Lismore, and it is difficult to imagine a more satisfying day than taking that ferry and spending time walking and exploring Lismore.

There is an old Gaelic song and poem:

Morvern for sword play, Mull for a song,
Appin's old sorrow, Lorne's rocky shore,
But give me a home, far o'er the foam,
My dear island home, Lismore.

And even the casual day visitor will be able to appreciate the sentiments of that song.

The best view, perhaps, on Lismore is obtained from the island's only hill, Barr Mor - *the Big Slope* - which only reaches a height of 417 feet, but affords an unparalleled vista of sea and mountain. The name of Lismore derives, probably from Lios Mor, or Great Garden, and the friendly limestone soil certainly provides most excellent grazing in its twelve miles of sea-girt length.

To the south of Lismore there is a skerry still known as Lady's Rock. A Maclean chief once marooned his unwanted Campbell wife there, so that she would be drowned by the incoming tide. However, she was rescued from her intended watery grave by a passing fishing boat, which took her off to Inveraray, centre of the Campbell power.

No doubt to his considerable chagrin, the Maclean chief met his supposedly dead wife one day when visiting Inveraray. He spent the next twelve months in some considerable discomfort in the dungeons of Inveraray castle, before meeting his own end at the hands of the Campbell executioner.

Continuing down the road back on the mainland, you come almost at once to the remarkable Castle Stalker, or, more properly *Stalchair* -- The Castle Of The Hunter.

Perhaps no other castle in the whole of Scotland has been the subject of more paintings and photographs, and none is more deserving. It is the very essence, the epitome, of Highland Romance. It stands on a rock off-shore at the mouth of Loch Luich, and can be reached only by boat. The original parts (the great nine feet thick walls) date from the 13th cent., and the upper parts from 1631. The landing place is a tiny inlet on the south-east side of the islet, but you cannot visit. It is a private residence, having been carefully and decently restored in recent years.

Like most Highland castles, Stalchair has had a sad and bloody history, too long and complicated to relate here. But you can find a taste of it all in the graveyard of Portnacroish, where a stone carries the inscription:-

> *1468. Above this spot was fought the bloody battle of Stalc, in which many hundreds fell, when the Stewarts and the MacLarens, their allies, in defence of Dugald, Chief of Appin, son of Sir John Stewart, Lord of Lorne and Innermeath, defeated the combined forces of the MacDougalls and the MacFarlanes.*

The Hollow of Treachery, nearby, is where most of the slaughter took place. When one reads the long history of death and destruction which make up the Highlands story, one can only be surprised that there were enough people left alive to suffer the final degradation of the Clearances.

Continuing north from Castle Stalchair, the cosy little island of Shuna lies just off shore, opposite Appin House, a not very attractive Georgian construction. Beyond, the road continues north to Balla-chulish and Fort William. Its main interest and it is a considerable interest is the view across Loch Linnhe to the mountains of Morvern, that vast, empty, glorious wasteland. You pass Beinn Bheither or Ben Vair, as it is spelled on the maps. That is the peak of the Thunderbolt. Glen Duror Forest clothes its lower slopes now, but cannot hide the splendour of the steep climb to 3361 feet in just two dramatic miles from sea level.

CAPITAL 'Q' FROM THE BOOK OF KELLS

OBAN AND DISTRICT

Oban has been called the Charing Cross of the North, but that certainly does it no justice. Of course, it is a centre of communications, with road, rail and sea connections. Indeed, one of the minor delights of being there is to watch the steamers depart for all the remote Hebrides. When the town of Oban was being built, the builders dug into the conglomerate rock and opened up unexpected caves which contained family groups of ancient skeletons, together with sea shells and other remains of people from seven thousand years ago. They were hunter-gatherers, and were some of the earliest people to settle on the mainland.

Oban lies in a deep bay, protected from gales by the island of Kerrera, a mile off shore. By sea, it can be approached only from north or south. It is certainly not an old town, and had no existence before the 18th cent. The first known reference to it as a separate place is in 1701, when the Customs authorities refer to as a 'creek'. And that is correct, for the name is derived from the Gaelic *Ob* meaning creek or bay, and the diminutive *an*.

It is a natural and well-sheltered harbour, and it seems was well used as such for trade up and down the Firth of Lorne, and gradually huts and houses were built, and a Customs House. There was an inn, too, and Duncan Ban MacIntyre, the Gaelic poet, spent carousing nights there with the landlady, a fervent anti- Jacobite. It was perhaps the lady's political views that caused that other great Gaelic poet Alasdair MacMhaighstir Alasdair, a profound Jacobite himself, to write so scathingly of Duncan Ban and of *Osdag Mhinorach an Obain* -- 'the shameless landlady of the Oban Inn'.

But the Highlands and Islands were opening up, books were

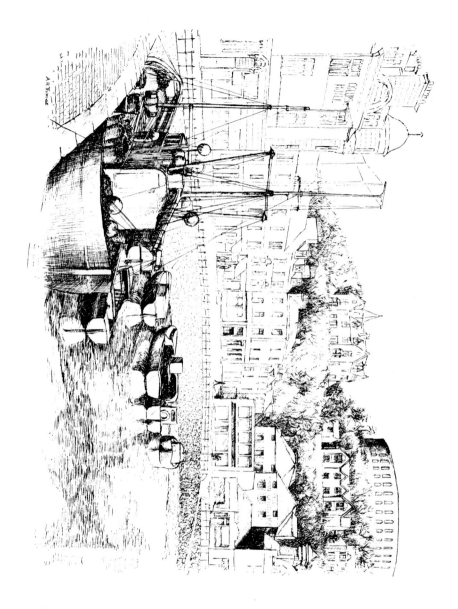

OBAN

being written about the Scottish 'wilderness' and intrepid travellers began finding their way north. In particular Pennant's *Journal* and James MacPherson's *Ossian* encouraged an influx of travellers. The tourist trade had begun, and has never ceased since.

Oban, what there was of it, was a natural centre, and flourished accordingly. Dr. Johnson and James Boswell landed there, and spent the night after arriving from Mull, and then rode on to Inverary. Their *Journey to the Western Isles* and Boswell's *Tour* undoubtedly added to the number of visitors.

But even then a town could not exist solely on providing for tourists. There were attempts at establishing industry as well as trade, and much credit for the foundation of Oban as a town rather than as a staging post must go to the Stevenson brothers, two lads brought up by their widowed mother in the 18th cent. One was a mason and the other a joiner, but their interests quickly spread in many directions, from boat building to brewing, and in most things they were successful.

John Stevenson died in 1869, aged 90, and by the time he died, Oban had become a considerable town. As early as 1835 five steamers called there regularly on their routes round the Hebrides. Most popular of those voyages was that to Iona and Staffa -- of Fingal's Cave fame -- and indeed these are probably still the most popular trips from Oban. And they well deserve to be. But Oban is the centre for the whole complicated web woven by Macbraynes steamers going regularly to the distant and tiny islands of the West. Cruising on those steamers, or island-hopping among the Hebrides, could well be the fullfillment of long-held dreams.

The arrival of the railway in 1880 allowed Oban to develop as a fishing port, with fishvans travelling direct to Southern markets. The railway allowed ordinary travellers to visit Oban, and not only those stout enough to brave the perils -- and undoubtedly there were perils -- of the roads.

Oban is a busy and working port, although today there are few boats fishing from the town itself. Still, every harbour is a pleasure

OBAN

to visit, and at Oban there is always something happening or something to watch.

The town is a fine, sheltered place, with hills on three sides and the island of Kerrera to seaward, but still there is no sense of being shut in. Just the same, every visitor should certainly go up Pulpit Hill and look at the view from there. Kerrera is a low island, and from Pulpit Hill you look right over it and out to Mull. To the north are the great hills and cliffs of Morvern. Be up there for a sunset, if you can. It is an experience never forgotten.

McCaig's Folly is a curious landmark. It is a great Colosseum-like erection on top of a hill overlooking the the town. It was started, but never finished, by John McCaig in 1897. He was a local banker, and, for very mixed reasons, decided to build his Colosseum as a museum. The windows, and there were to be many of them, were to have held statues of his relatives. Don't be too hard on the memory of John McCaig. The Folly was not just a memorial to an ego, but was also a genuine attempt to help the unemployed of the area. Although perhaps not particularly beautiful by day, the floodlit Folly by night is a fine sight.

If you stay in Oban (and it is an excellent centre), surely you will take the passenger ferry to Kerrara. Although so close to the mainland, it still has that indefinable sense of being an island, and indeed is a fine one. It is about five miles long and of two miles breadth. Just big enough to be well explored in a day.

Gylen Castle, at the south-west of the island, is stark and dramatic. It was a stronghold of the MacDougalls of Lorne, and was burned and pillaged by General Leslie's army in the 17th cent., not so long after it was built, for it dates only from the 16th cent. The castle rises stark from the cliffs on three sides, and the fourth side is protected by an outer wall. It was not large, only about 20 feet by 50 feet, but is still imposing, facing the open sea and protected by cliffs.

It was during the pillaging and burning of the castle by General Leslie's troops that the famous Brooch of Lorne was lost, and remained lost for 180 years. That was during the terrible days of Civil War, when the Covenanter Army of Scotland and the English Parliamentary Army fought against the forces of the King. General Leslie commanded the Covenanting troops. The Brooch of Lorne belonged to King Robert Bruce. I have already told the tale, but it bears repeating, as does anything about The Bruce. One day the King was travelling near Tyndrum, during his struggles to establish a State covering the whole of Scotland. He was in enemy territory, and was confronted by a trio of his enemies. It was a hard fought contest, but Robert Bruce escaped. He left behind the brooch which had secured his cloak, and he left it clutched in the hand of a severed MacDougall arm.

The brooch was kept by the MacDougalls in Gylen Castle, but was lost at the sacking of the castle. Eventually it reappeared and, generously, was returned to the MacDougalls, and today is preserved in the MacDougall mansion house near Dunollie castle at Oban.

The highest point of Kerrara is only 600 feet above the sea, and for the small effort of climbing there, one is rewarded with a remarkable vista of sea, mountains, sky and islands. In which ever direction you turn, there is beauty unsurpassed. Morvern, Ardgour, Cruachan, Nevis, the Paps of Jura, Mull, all reach skyward: Seil island, Scarba island and many others bejewel the sea. A sight of great magnificence indeed.

There are two fine castles in the immediate environs of Oban, Dunollie and Dunstaffnage, both very interesting.

Dunstaffnage castle stands on a small peninsula -- rather ugly and built up these days -- between Connnel and Oban on the A816. Built in the 13th cent., it is a great ruin today, but still grim and impressive.

Dunstaffnage and its near neighbour Dunollie, at Oban itself, were meant to guard the Firth of Lorne. They were MacDougall strongholds. Dunstaffnage is built on a solid rock headland, and its foundations spring like the trunk of some mighty tree from the rock contours. There is a great curtain wall, more than 100 yards long, surrounding the whole, and that wall is 24 feet high and nine feet thick. There are two round towers on the walls, and one of those towers is the castle keep -- the final place of defence if the curtain wall was breached. Outside the curtain wall is the chapel, built at the same time as the castle.

The chapel is a delight, being, it has been written, '*one of the richest and finest examples of early First Pointed Gothic in Scotland, and is not exceeded in vigour and grace by any other like piece of architecture in the kingdom.*' The 'early pointed' refers to the arches which the craftsmen of the 13th cent. had learned to lighten and elongate, after the sturdy roundness of Norman architecture.

Robert Bruce, before whom no castle was safe, captured Dunstaffnage in 1308, and from then on it seemed that Dunstaffnage was at the centre of much of Scotland's history.

James IV was there in 1493, and James V used it as a naval base in 1531. It was at Dunstaffnage that the plot was laid to kill

Campbell of Cawdor in 1592. And so on through history. Flora MacDonald, the lassie who helped Prince Charles Edward escape by dressing him as her maid and thus passing the English searchers, was held for ten days in Dunstaffnage after her arrest and before being moved on for trial in London. Her bravery must have struck some sort of romantic chord, though, for she went virtually unpunished for her 'treachery', whilst many others died vilely on the gallows.

Dr. Douglas Simpson has written a definitive history of Dunstaffnage, and he identifies that castle as the one described by Smollett in his *Humphrey Clinker*, a description that tells us much about life in the many Scottish castles of the day. It seems, according to Humphrey Clinker, that Mr. Campbell, the laird, detested the bagipes, but tradition dictated that the hereditary piper play for an hour each morning and the laird had to stuff his ears with wool to withstand the torment.

One of many fascinating records about Dunstaffnage relates that James I held a court of 'Pleadings' there about 1431. The results were briefly summarised:

'Some of the misdemeanants he pardoned; others he admonished; a few he blessed, and a lot he hanged.'

Dunollie Castle is right at the entrance to Oban Bay, at the north end. There is not too much of it left today, for the old castle was used as a convenient quarry (like so many others) when the MacDougalls decided that the time had come to vacate its bleakness and build a new mansion house close by. That was in about 1746, when the idea that old things and places were precious had not yet developed, and it was felt that progress was all.

It is a pity that the old castle has been so despoiled, for it was very ancient indeed. As long ago as 686 the Annals of Ulster mention a castle of Dunollie. It, like Dunstaffnage, was a MacDougall castle, and that is a very ancient line, tracing back to Lorne, the brother of Fergus who founded the kingdom of Dalriada.

Sir Walter Scott wrote about the old castle, and so did William Wordsworth, who visited it during his Highland tour with sister

Dorothy and friend Coleridge. Wordsworth wrote of a captured eagle he saw at the castle:

> *Dishonoured rock and ruin that, by law*
> *Tyrannic, keep the Bird of Jove embarred*
> *Like a lone criminal whose life is spared.*
> *Vexed is he, and screams aloud.*

Two years later he visited the castle again. The caged eagle was gone, but he wrote about a crude mosaic he saw there, of an eagle with outstretched wings. That mosaic, in rounded white pebbles, could still be seen there until recently.

Hard by the castle is the present mansion house of the MacDougalls, and the Brooch of Lorne is there. It is surmounted by a large and curious crystal, which always glows warmly as though with an interior fire. There are a number of pearls set in a circle round the crystal, and the centre unscrews to disclose a small box which once, it is said, contained a fragment of bone, (probably a saintly relic), and a piece of ancient MacDougall tartan.

Dunollie is one of the few castles that General Leslie failed to take in 1647, and in the Jacobite rising of 1715, when the laird was out with the Jacobites, the castle was successfully defended by the

Laird's wife.

The MacDougall estates and castles were forfeited to the Crown after 1715, but were restored in 1727, and the Laird, who had been all those years living the life of a fugitive (for part of the time in a cave on the shores of Loch Feochan), returned to his castle.

In 1745, the new young Laird ached to join his Prince whose standard had been raised at Glenfinnan, but his young wife poured a kettle of boiling water over his feet so that he could not join that ill-fated rising. Tough ladies, those MacDougalls.

Barcaldine Castle is the last of the three castles near Oban. This very good example of a 16th cent. tower house is necessarily approached through the sort of modern muddle that seems inseparable from any Highland development.

Leave the main road north (A828) out of Oban by taking the minor road to the left after crossing the bridge at Conell. This area is Benderloch, and Barcaldine Castle sits on the great hammer-like headland protruding into the Lynn of Lorne, washed to the north by Loch Creran and to the south by the waters of Ardmuchnish Bay.

If you press on bravely through the mess of 'development' you will find several very interesting historical sites. There is a very early fort here, which some have identified as Ptolemy's *Beregonium*. There are a few remains of a vitrified fort, *Dun Mhic Uisneachan*, or the Fort Of The Sons of Uisneach, that is, the Fingalians.

These vitrified forts are strange. As the name implies, they are made of vitrified rock, or, in fact, of glass! There are many of them throughout the Highlands, and their origin is a mystery.

There is no mystery about how they became vitrified, though. They were built of silica-bearing stones embedded in brushwood and peat, and the brushwood was fired, perhaps by accident, or perhaps intentionally. The resultant great heat melted the silica into a form of glass. Don't expect something like the Crystal Palace, though. These ruins are very old, and today consist of nothing more than lines of glassy stones almost lost amongst the scrub.

The whole of this little headland well repays exploration, even though it has, in part, been raped by the developers. There are several burial cairns and standing stones, memorials to a time long past. There is a bridge to the island of Eriska to the north, and in the spring of the year, the island is a riot of rhododendrons.

Barcaldine Castle itself, now restored to good condition, gleams white on its eminence above the shore. And that is strange, for it was once known as The Black Castle. 'L' shaped, and of three stories, with a stair-tower and angle-turrets, the walls are pierced by several strategically placed holes for guns.

There is evidence that it was a fine dwelling house as well as a defensive position. The drawing room off the main hall is comfortably panelled, and, for its day, a cosy place. Of course, not all guests at the castle enjoyed those amenities. There is a ferocious bottle-neck dungeon in the basement.

Barcaldine was a Campbell castle, originally built by Duncan Campbell of Glenorchy, but it passed into the hands of an illegitimate son, Para Beg, who seems to have bred prolifically. Most of Para Beg's descendants were military men, but there was one minister amongst them who remained in charge of Ardchattan Parish for sixty-one years, twenty-seven as an Episcopalian and thirty-four as a minister of the Church of Scotland. After his own abandonment of Episcopalianism, he was a forthright enemy of all bishops, and there is an account of him, kilt-clad, sword in one hand and pistol in the other, travelling all the way to remote Ardnamurchan to force a Presbyterian minister onto a very reluctant Episcopalian congregation.

Not far away from Barcaldine is a factory which turns seaweed into a curious host of industrial products. You may not know it, but seaweed is used in many things, from beer to fruit jellies. This factory, one of two in Scotland, is in fact a poignant reminder of one of the many tragedies of Highland economy.

A vital constituent of explosives can be manufactured from seaweed, and the vast kelp fields of the Highlands and Islands are a rich source of seaweed. During the Napoleonic wars, imports of this material for explosives were cut off, and a considerable Highland industry of kelp gathering and burning developed, with the lairds encouraging their tenants to neglect the land and concentrate on gathering kelp and burning it to the required ash on the beaches. Not that the peasants, the cottars and crofters got rich from this, although the lairds and factors did.

Came the end of the wars, and imports again became available. There was an immediate collapse of the local industry, for, true to tradition, there had been no attempt to produce the ash by economical methods -- why bother, when labour was so cheap and plentiful? The cottars and the crofters had to return again to their neglected and run-down bits of land, struggling to restore its fertility, and greatly hampered in this because the seaweed, their only fertiliser, was no longer so freely available.

Looking at this very area today, with its sadly neglected land, its waving fields of Bed And Breakfast signs, one wonders about the future. A reiterated lesson of history is that any country which neglects its land, and the fertility of that land, while searching for quick financial returns, is walking the edge of a precipice over which many have fallen.

Leaving the headland on which Barcaldine stands, one is back in Benderloch proper. Instead of just going along that main road, it is suggested that you leave the road just by Connel Bridge and wander off through the back roads of Gleann Salach.

After leaving the shores of Loch Etive, the road climbs 500 steep feet to the head of the pass, and a halt there to look back at the Loch winding far below is well worth while. The great sweep of Ben Cruachan, all 3600 feet of it, lifts sharply across the Loch, and to the east and north there is the whole vast emptiness of Scotland's highest mountains. A great sight at any time.

Ardchattan Priory is on the shore of Loch Etive. It is a private house now, but still incorporates the ancient monastery. It was founded there in 1230, for the Valliscaulian Order, and named for St. Catan. In 1309 Robert Bruce held a National Council there, the last

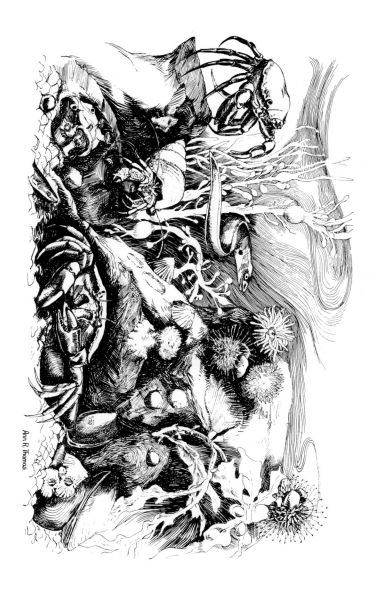

ROCK POOL

such Council to be conducted in Gaelic. Cromwell's troops burned the building in 1654, but what remains are open to the public. There are some fine examples of First Pointed work and an eleventh century cross.

Archattan was one of three Valliscaulian Priories in Scotland, and that was a very strict Order. There were seven services every day, and total silence had to be maintained between the services. No meat was allowed, and the monks had to wear hair shirts day and night. The Priory fell into disrepair after the Dissolution, but the Refectory is now a private house, part of which is open to the public, and well worth seeing. People have eaten in that room every day for seven hundred years.

The Priory ruins are delightful, and so are the tombs. There is one tomb of the MacDougalls. Two brothers MacDougall were Priors at Ardchattan, and they are shown in their monastic dress, while between them is a corpse with a toad gnawing at its vitals. The mother and father of the Priors, and another brother, are there too, with the men in armour of different periods, and the lady in a fashionable headdress with a veil. It is a grand tomb, and there are others, perhaps not so grand, but certainly interesting.

Nearby, but back on the main road north, is the Sea Life Centre. It is not often you have the chance to see all the many varieties of fish which swarm round our coasts. At the Centre you can see them, all alive and close up, and in all their many shapes and sizes. Very interesting indeed.

About two miles south of Oban, on A816, a minor road on the right leads to Kilbride and on to the lonely shores of Loch Feochan.

About a mile after leaving the major road, there is the Kilbride Cross, or alternatively the Campbell of Lerag Cross, a lovely Celtic cross about eleven feet high, and intricately carved. A dragon is there, surrounded by floral decoration, but the central scene is a Crucifixion. The date '1516' is cut into the stone at the foot of the Cross. It is a lovely thing, and by itself well worthy of a visit. But there is more.

Close by there is the unroofed ruin of the old Kilbride Parish Church with a walled churchyard and the burial ground of the MacDougalls, and a fine quiet place it is. The Kilbride Cross itself was re-erected in 1926. It had been lying on the ground in three pieces, possibly overthrown by some of the *unco guid* during the Reformation, as so many others were.

Another fine excursion from Oban (and it would be a pity to miss it) is the quiet drive on the minor road betwen Oban and Taynuilt, via Strantoiler and Clachadow, and through Glen Lonan. At the east end of Loch Lonan, tiny and quiet in the hills, there are two forts, overgrown and unexcavated, but still very clear.

Just about a mile west of Glenmachried, and very obvious, is the twelve foot high standing stone where, legend tells us, the Ossianic hero Diarmid died slaying the boar. To be honest, there is rather more evidence that the boar and Diarmid did not die here, but much further south, on the Hill of the Boar, in Kintyre. The whole road is one of delight and quietness, and very much worth while.

South of Oban again, on the Lochgilphead road (A816), it is

very worth while side-tracking to the Craignish Peninsula.

Turn left on to B8002 about 2 miles after leaving the shores of Loch Melford. This arrowhead of a peninsula is perhaps best visited in May and June, when the gardens of Craignish Castle are open to the public. They are an astonishing wealth of rhododendrons in all possible colours and varieties, and were laid out originally by Osgood Mackenzie, best known for his creation of Inverewe Gardens in Wester Ross.

Craignish is the site of a very old building, although nothing now remains of the original. The present building is 16th cent.

Go in past the castle to the end of the road, and then continue walking to the end of the track at Craignish Point. This is Dorus Mor, the Great Gate, between Craignish and Garbh Reisa Island.

When the tide is setting, the sea is a menacing swirl, patterned with dangerous-looking small whirlpools. In spite of the menacing appearance, it is generally safe enough for boats, but that is certainly not true of the dreaded Corrrievrechan, that roaring menace between Jura and Scarba, about 4 miles off Craignish, and easily seen and heard from there.

The tide floods up the Sound of Jura then turns sharply westwards into the Gulf of Corrievrechan, travelling at a smart nine knots or so. In the Gulf the waters strike a great submerged rock pyramid, and the resulting upheaval can be seen and heard for miles. A bard described it as the *the roaring of a thousand chariots.*

In its publication *The West Coast of Scotland Pilot*, The Admiralty states: 'Navigation is at times most hazardous and no stranger under any circumstances can be justified in attempting it.'

It is a great whirlpool, and it has caused the loss of even large and powerful ships. If the wind is westerly against the tide and blowing fresh, the roaring of the waters is even more loud and threatening. The name Corrievrechan is properly Coire Breacain, or Speckled Corrie, and comes from the appearance of the foam-flecked waters.

The little Craignish peninsula, and from there to the south, running down to Loch Crinan and the Crinan Canal, is very rich with standing stones, duns, and other memorials to a distant past. The islands of Seil and Luing are easily reached from Oban, and are well worth while visiting. Go south from Oban on A816 to Kilninver, where the road leaves the shores of Loch Feochan. Take the minor road on the right. A little further on this road forks, with the right fork going south to Ardmaddy Castle, which is really no castle at all, but a rather graceful 18th century house.

The left hand fork leads to the island of Seil, via the Bridge Over The Atlantic. This shapely structure was built in 1791, and really does cross at least an arm of the Atlantic Ocean, joining Seil Island and the mainland. The builder was one of the Stevensons, who also built most of Oban, and he built well and gracefully, with enough height over the water that the sailing ships of the day could pass under. He built it, of course, for horse and foot traffic, but it just as eaily bears the heavy loads of today.

Just over the bridge is an inn, Tigh an Truish, or, strangely, House of the Trousers. And thereby hangs a tale. After the uprising of 1745, the Highlanders were forbidden to wear their traditional plaid or kilt, and the men had to dress in the despised trousers of the Lowlands and England. Then, as indeed now, half-baked laws from the south are properly scorned in the remote parts of Scotland, and the men of Seil continued to wear their plaids and kilts when on the island. When going to the mainland, though, they had to obey that stupid law, and changed into trousers at the inn, while no doubt having a welcome 'refreshment' at the same time. Hence the name, which is kept to this day.

You have the choice, having crossed the Atlantic, of going to Easdale or south again to the island of Luing by Cuan Ferry.

Easdale island, just off-shore, was once a busy industrial centre, in the days when slates were used on every building. Interestingly, the slate beds were under high water mark, and when the tide was low and work could be done, dry wooden wedges were driven into the slate. When the tide came in and covered the work place, the water made the wedges swell, and the slate was split. But that was four hundred years ago. Later, walls were built and pumps used to keep the sea away from the workings, and blasting powder did the splitting. Just over a hundred years ago, eleven million slates a year were coming from Easdale. It all ended in 1881, one dark winter night of hellish gales when the sea walls were breached and the quarries flooded. They never recovered from that blow, although some slates continued to be produced for another fifty years or so.

The i.aland become a desolation of empty houses and buildings. Today, it is different. Time and nature have worked their familiar miracle, and Easdale Island is again a thriving little commuity, and a pretty one, with the quarry workings now fascinating deep sea pools, and with shrubs and flowers cloaking the old buildings. Go there for the sheer pleasure of being on that so remote, yet so accessible little island, but also visit the Folk Museum and learn more about a most unusual history.

Luing Island, further south, was once held to be the best arable land in the whole of Lorne, but that is no great praise. It was once a crowded little island, with every possible yard of ground cultivated. That came to an end in the 1850's, when the Clearances came to Luing, and the people were moved out, but this time to make way for cattle, not sheep, for Lord Breadalbane, the proprietor, was a renowned cattle breeder. And he hardly needed the families any more, for their chief value had been as a source of fighting men and they were no longer needed in the 19th century.

Luing is still a cattle island, and a new breed has been evolved there, that, predictably, is called the Luing. It is a cross between the Highlander and the Shorthorn. This new breed combines the beef quality of the Shorthorn and the hardiness of the Highlander, and is proving very successful.

There have been some remarkable characters on Luing, but perhaps none so strange as Alex. Campbell. He disapproved of almost everything in the whole world and quarrelled with most things. There is a ruined church at Kilchattan on Luing where Alex. carved his messages of disapproval to be seen by all, he hoped, for all eternity. Amongst other things, he disapproved of:-

..........*I leave my testimony against the Church of England......
the Church of Scotland.....my brother Duncan Campbell. Duncan
Clark in saying that my brother's cow was not pushing
mine.....against George III.....play actors and pictures...dancing*

schools...the low country .....women that wear Babylonish garments, that are rigged out with stretched necks, tinkling as they go..... gentlemen.....parasols.....men that have whiskers......'

The Garvellachs, the Islands of the Sea, can be seen from both Seil and Luing, and a grand island-studded scene they make, out to the west. They are uninhabited, of course, but there are very ancient ruins of chapels and monks' cells. Tradition holds that St. Columba's mother is buried on one of those islands.

The Salmon Centre, about 7 miles south of Oban on the A816, makes an interesting visit. You cannot have failed to notice the large number of fish farms in the various sea lochs: here is an opportunity to inspect one. You can see the whole process of rearing the salmon, and also learn about the life-cycle of that superb migratory fish which is now reared in such large quantities in these waters. There is a salmon pool with an under-water window, which allows you to see the fish in something like their natural conditions. And, incidentally, you can also eat well there.

DALMALLY

Coming from the south, you are likely to approach Dalmally by the direct road (A855) from Tyndrum. It is a pleasant enough road, but it is much better to carry on north a little way from Tyndrum (A82) to just south of Bridge of Orchy, where B8074 turns off to the left. Follow that road down the Glen of Orchy. It is a fine, twisting road, following the river with its many cascades. The views of mountains near and far are lovely. For all its beauties, though, Glen Orchy is a sad and haunted place.

Once, not so long ago, it was a populated and well-farmed glen. Indeed, it could be so again. But Lord Breadalbane cleared the people off the land in the 19th cent. to install sheep, that 'White Plague' which killed so many communities and people. Today, of course, the sheep have gone, in their turn, and forestry clothes the hills in trees, hiding the ruined houses and villages.

The bridge at Dalmally is an interesting memento of the past, for it was built in 1799 for the convenience of the cattle drovers taking their great herds of black cattle to the trysts at Falkirk and Crieff. Those were the days when great herds of cattle from all the islands and Highlands were driven south to the cattle markets and finally to satisfy the hunger of the growing masses in the big English cities. Those once fertile glens which produced such vast herds of cattle are empty now, and lovely in their desolation, and it is hard to realise that as late as 1850 as many as 150,000 cattle came out of these glens and from the islands, and were were sold at the thrice-yearly sales.

Dalmally Church is well worth a visit. It is only 18th cent., but the octagonal shape is very unusual, and is surmounted by a square

HEAD OF LOCH AWE & KILCHURN CASTLE

tower and clock. The churchyard has some interesting stones, and the nearby Manse was designed by Telford, that ubiquitous man.

There is a lovely story about one of the ministers of Dalmally Church -- not the present building but an earlier one. The Minister was an Episcopalian, and after the final triumph of Presbyterianism, the kirk synod sent one of their own kind to replace him. They had not reckoned on the congregation. The Church of Scotland might have rejected Episcopalianism, but the people of Dalmally were determined to keep their Episcopalian minister. The new man, when he went to the church to take it over, was met by his congregation with drawn swords and they, with a piper playing 'The March of Death', escorted him to the parish boundary and extorted a promise that never again would he enter the parish. He kept his word, and the old Episcopalian minister kept his charge for thirty five more years.

Today, that is no more than a pleasant little story, but behind it, in the history of the Covenanters, is an episode of history that rent Scotland apart, cost unknown thousands of lives and left a legacy of bitterness that troubles Scotland even today. To us, it seems a remote and indeed rather stupid theological quarrel of no importance. To our forefathers it was of such importance that they were well prepared to die for their version of God-given truth.

The great gloomy remains of Kilchurn Castle stand on the banks of Loch Awe, hard by Dalmally. This was one of the major strongholds of the Campbells of Glen Orchy, whose lands once stretched from Luing to Loch Tay in the east. It was an island castle, but over the centuries a strand of shingle has been deposited which now links it to the shore. Colin Campbell built Kilchurn in 1440, and, perhaps because of its great size and impregnable position, it had a reasonably quiet life, although the Royalists unsuccessfully tried to take it in 1653. In 1770 the roof was removed and the fabric left to moulder quietly away. Wordsworth was impressed by Kilchurn, and wrote:-

> Child of a loud-throated war, the mountain stream
> Roars in thy hearing; but thy hour of rest

Is come, and thou art silent in thy age,
Save when the winds sweep by.....

Not perhaps poetry of a very high order, but none of the verse
he wrote about the Highlands was of much note; he seemed to find it
difficult to adjust to the scale of Highland grandeur.

There is a legend that Colin Campbell, when crusading in the
Holy Land, had a dream that his house, Kilchurn, was in danger, and
that he must return at once. He did so, and on approaching Kilchurn,
found that there were sounds of revelry and mirth, for a wedding
was to be held that day. His wife was to be married to the local
Baron, one McCorquodale. He, like wicked barons else-where (and I
wonder why all Barons seem, in legend, to be wicked? -- Lords
seldom are, and Princes never!) had been persuading the Lady that
her husband was dead, and had carefully waylaid and killed all the
messengers Colin had sent. Now the wicked deed was to be
consummated.

But Colin Campbell, as a new guest at the castle, had to be
refreshed, so meat and wine were called for. Colin, though, insisted
that only the Lady should serve the wine, and she did. (Colin must
have had a bad time crusading, for she did not recognise him.) Colin
drained the cup of wine, and quietly slipped his wedding ring into the
empty cup before handing it back to his wife. She recognised the
ring, if not her husband, and so the wicked Baron was foiled, as they
usually are, in legend if not in reality.

In Dalmally itself, just where B8077 branches off, is the
curiously shaped Bruce's Stone. It is not clear why it is so called,
although Robert Bruce passed that way twice, once after his
temporary defeat at Methvin in 1306 and again in 1308 on his way to
the victory at the Pass of Brander.

The village of Cladich is not far from Dalmally, on the main
Inverary-Oban road (A819). The view from Cladich, although
somewhat marred by eletricity pylons, is still magnificent, with Ben
Cruachan dominating everything, and as you travel along Loch Awe
the headlands and islands in the Loch are unforgettable in their

beauty.

The Loch is ringed by great peaks, many of them over the magic 3000 feet mark, which means that they are 'Munros', and so the climbing target of the 'Munro-baggers'. Adding to the beauty, the mountains are pierced by fine rivers. Inishail Island, with its very ancient burial ground, lies off-shore. Inishail, the 'Island of Rest', has many fine old carved stones of the 14th and 15th cents. In the old days, of course, wolves abounded in Scotland, and important people were buried on islands to protect the graves from them. The great forests of the Highlands were often fired in order to drive out wolves or enemies and that contributed to the denudation of these hills, once clothed in native hardwoods, but now, at best, buried under the scowling phalanxes of Forestry Commission conifers.

A truly fine expedition is to hire a boat on Loch Awe and explore some of the little islands. There is Inishail itself, and Fraoch Eilean with the ruin of a very early castle standing most impressively on a crag. Fraoch Eilean is a picture of delight in spring, when it is clad with wild flowers.

The castle is a Campbell property, and was given to that family by Robert Bruce, who soundly defeated its previous owners at the battle fought in the nearby Pass of Brander. Its particular importance is that it is the last surviving Norman period castle in Scotland, although measuring only about 60 feet by 30 feet.

The name 'Fraoch Eilean' would normally mean Heather Island, but no heather grows there. Once, though, long ago, some berries did grow on the island, the berries of everlasting youth, and they were guarded by an awesome dragon. In one version of the legend, a young man, Fraoch, succeeded in killing the dragon and collecting some berries. Alas, though, all was not well, for Fraoch had been sent on his quest by a woman, not his love, but the mother of his love, and neither his intentions nor hers were pure. So he died of his wounds, and she died because the berries poisoned her. So, if you eat berries on Eilean Fraoch take care that your wish for the life eternal is for good reasons!

Another version holds that it was the Golden Fruit of Immortality that grew there, guarded by a great viper, and that none who had tried to pluck the fruit had returned -- all had perished from the poison and the enveloping coils of the serpent.

Fraoch loved the maid Mego, and loved her so deeply that he desired immortality for her, even if it should cost him his own life, and even though he had to brave the serpent. He tried to pluck the fruit, and he and the serpent fought a bitter battle after which both lay dead. But as the serpent died, so did the Golden Fruit wither, and Mego died, too, of sorrow, so that she and her love were reunited.

Whether you believe either or neither of these legends, the island remains an important centre in Celtic mythology.

If you venture on to Loch Awe, do watch out for *Beathach Mor Loch Obha* --The Great Beast of Loch Awe. This is a great water-beast of some sort, although, true enough, it has not been sighted in recent centuries. It was (perhaps is) a strange cross between a horse and an enormous eel, and with twelve legs. It was much bigger and much more ferocious than that puny creature in Loch Ness. When the Loch froze, the Beathach Mor always came to the surface, and smashed up the ice, so that the people round about heard the great crashing and groaning and rumbling.

On the minor road between Achlian and Dalmally there is a memorial to Duncan Ban MacIntyre (1724-1812), one of the most celebrated Gaelic poets. He was a game keeper on Black Mount, and had a stupendous knowledge of the old oral traditions of poetry in the language he loved. His poems, which are still read and enjoyed, are great paeans of praise for the mountains he knew so well, and the animals, especially the deer, which lived on them.

Duncan Ban had an interesting and long life. He lived to the age of 88 and became a poet almost by accident. He was 21 at the time of the 1745 rising, and foolishly agreed to take the place of a neighbouring tacksman who had been called to the Argyll Militia -- the King's men. Duncan was promised 300 marks (if he returned from the wars) and was loaned a sword. But his heart was not in it, for indeed he was at least half a Jacobite, and at the battle of Falkirk he lost the sword, and, it seems, displayed neither courage nor energy. Returning home he asked for payment and not surprisingly was refused. So he wrote his first poem, a bitter complaint against the tacksman, who was certainly not amused. Duncan Ban received a beating as payment for that poem, but it set him firmly into the path of poetry, and during his long lifetime he had three volumes of poetry published -- all in Gaelic, for he had no English.

Do make the short climb to the elaborate monument erected to Duncan Ban, and you will be rewarded by a fine view over the best part of Loch Awe. You will see Kilchurn Castle from a different angle, and that alone would be worth the little effort, and the islands bejewelling the loch are lovely.

The Castle itself, like Castle Stalker in Appin, is a favourite subject for painters and photographers. It was built in the early 15th cent. by the Campbells of Glen Orchy. It seems to rise straight out of the water, with a fine square keep, and walls still at their full height. Grand and romantic though the ruin is, it is the setting of great glens and mountains that complete this picture.

Close by, near the little house of Ardteatle, is one of the most mysterious places in Scotland. It is a stone circle, but the stones are boulders, not square nor worked in any way. In the middle of those sixteen boulders is another great erratic boulder, split into three parts, and with every surface covered by cup-marks and circular holes. The purpose of this massive human effort so long ago is quite unknown, and one can only stand and wonder about it.

LOCH AWE NORTH SIDE

Travelling towards Oban from Dalmally, the road (A85) continues on the north side of Loch Awe through the dramatic Pass of Brander, where road and rail cling precariously together, at times overhanging the narrow neck of the Loch and its river outlet.

It was here, at the Pass of Brander, that King Robert Bruce won one of those spectacular victories that have made his campaigns text-books for guerilla fighters in many countries to this day. That was in 1308, when the King was intent on crushing the turbulent chiefs, especially the MacDougalls.

He and his ally Sir James Douglas were planning to go through the Pass of Brander into MacDougall territory, and this seemed an ideal chance for a MacDougall final victory. Their men were hidden on the heights above the pass ready to ambush the King. It was exactly the same tactic that Robert Bruce had used himself a year earlier to inflict a terrible defeat on the English Army far to the south at Loch Trool in Ayrshire. He was certainly not going to be caught by that sort of ambush.

Sir James Douglas and his men were sent far out to the wing and to the very top of Ben Cruachan. When the King and his men began moving through the pass, great boulders were sent hurtling down on them by the MacDougall men. Immediately, the King's swiftest and most lightly armed men were sent racing up the hill to meet the MacDougalls, who found themselves pincered between those panting warriors and the archers of Douglas coming down the hill. They died, and the King went on his way to besiege and take Dunstaffnage Castle, destroy the power of the MacDougalls and give much of their land to Campbell of Lochawe, his friend and ally, with

A power station at work.

For more details see inside.

Everyday, up until mid October, you can go underground and see Cruachan Hydro Power Station at work. Visit the huge turbine halls, where water is drawn down 364 metres from the reservoir above. On the way you'll see plants actually growing out of the walls, an unexpected product of the light and heating systems we use.

So where will you find Britain's most unusual power station? At Loch Awe on the A85, just 15 miles from Oban.

Come along, have a look around our shop and visitors' centre and we'll fill in all the details.

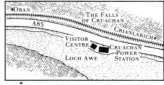

✴ ScottishPower

OPEN: *9am to 4.30pm.* FREE CAR PARK
TOURS: ADULTS £1.80. CHILDREN 50p
CHILDREN *under 8* FREE. TEL: 086 62 673.

results that Robert Bruce could not know, but that left indelible marks on Scottish history.

Loch Awe was itself made by a witch, of course. Certainly, it was an accident, and she tried to empty all the water out of the fertile valley, but failed. It happened this way. The Cailleach Bheur, from the island of Mull, was a witch. She had only one eye, but she was very big, so big indeed that she had no trouble wading over the Sound of Mull, for the water came barely to her knees. She did a lot of wading, it seems, for one day, when she was carrying a creel of stones somewhere off the west coast, some of them fell into the sea, and became the Hebrides.

Anyway, she was staying on the Mull of Kintyre, but the grazing there was not good enough for her favourite cow, so every day she and her cow went up to Ben Cruachan, where there was some good grass. She used to rest on the Ben, by a magic well which was covered by a huge granite slab, which she removed every day -- it was no effort for her -- to allow her cow to drink. But it *was* a magic well, and she knew that if the slab was not replaced every day before sunset, so much water would gush out that the whole world might be drowned.

All went well, but one day, a fine day of sunshine, the Cailleach Bheur fell asleep on her grassy hillock, and slept all through the day and after the sun had set. As it disappeared over the distant sea, there was a great roar, and water tumbled out of the well in an enormous torrent. This woke the witch, and using her best magic she got the great granite slab back on to the well, and stopped the flow, but not before the lovely valley below her had been filled by the water. She tried her witch-like best to get all that water to flow back into the magic well, but could not do it. And that is how Loch Awe came into being.

Ben Cruachan, the great hill to the north of the Loch's narrow tongue, contains real wonders, greater than anything ever performed by the Cailleach Bheur.

That mountain has been hollowed by man's hand, and in a

great cavern as big as a cathedral there is a vast generating station, of which not a sign is visible from outside. It is a pumped storage system, in which the waters of Loch Awe are pumped high up the mountain to a reservoir up there. The pumping is done at night when there is little demand for electricity. Then during the day the waters run back, powering the turbines that drive the generators and produce electricity. Noiseless, smokeless, harmless, and quite risk-free. You are welcome to visit there, and see for yourself. Visiting a power station on your holiday may seem a strange thing to do, but this power station is exceptional (and the views quite magnificent from the top of the mountain).

LOCH ETIVE FROM BEN CRUACHAN

Loch Awe is of course a salmon loch, but as part of the hydro-electricity scheme (the only part visible) a small dam has been built where the loch becomes a river leading to Loch Etive and eventually to the sea. It is up that river that the salmon and seatrout must travel on their way to spawn in the rivers that feed Loch Awe. They cannot jump the dam, and so a lift has been installed for their convenience, and you can stop there and watch, if the time is right, fine fresh-run fish going up the height of the dam in their own lift. Electric powered, of course.

On the shore of the loch, and before you reach the Pass of Brander, there is the quite charming St. Conan's Church, looking out to Fraoch Eilean. It is a delight; do stop and look at it.

It was built at the end of last century by Walter Campbell, the local laird, on the site of a much older building. Walter Campbell was his own architect, and all the work was done by local craftsmen. The main theme of the building is Romanesque, but Walter Campbell utilised every possible architectural form and design. Sometimes the results are remarkably harmonious and sometimes they clash hilariously. However, the overall effect is strangely beautiful. Walter Campbell missed nothing -- massive flying buttresses, Roman, Norman and Gothic arches, even a small cloister, a Saxon tower, gargoyles -- it is all there, like illustrations in some fantastic text book of architecture. There is the Bruce Chapel, with a wooden effigy of King Robert, with alabaster face and hands, lit by a charming window, and below the effigy a fragment of bone brought from Bruce's grave at Dunfermline.

So, St. Conan's Church, that strange example of architectural kleptomania, really has everything, and a description probably makes it sound brash and vulgar. Surprisingly, it is not like that at all, and although it certainly raises a smile, there is still a sense of dignity and achievement about it. Very much worth visiting.

Soon, the river Awe empties into Loch Etive at Bonawe. There are some very interesting ruins here, not of ancient churches or castles, but of quite recent iron smelting works. There are no local deposits of iron ore, and this was brought all the way from Cumbria, but there was plenty of wood to make charcoal to fire the furnaces, and plenty of water power to work the bellows.

This was not the only iron smelting plant in the Highlands by any means, and to some considerable extent they were responsible for the destruction of the natural forest cover. It takes a lot of wood to smelt iron, and the natural fir, oak, beech and birch woods round Loch Etive and far afield were denuded. They must have been a sight far finer than today's ranks of conifers.

Close by Bonawe a minor road (B845) runs off to the south, and by following this you can regain the north shore of Loch Awe. Do take that road; it is a delight, especially in the spring of the year.

The area quite clearly was a centre of civilisation long ago, for it is littered with ancient standing stones (many now fallen) and ancient chapels or Cils. The place names are indicative -- Kilvaree, Kilmaronaig, Cilchorril, Kilcherenon -- all places where early Christians settled in the dawn of history.

The road runs steeply up Glen Nant, past Tailor's Leap, where once a tailor escaped the excisemen by leaping across a chasm they dare not attempt. If you want to find utter peace and solitude, take the tiny track to the right, leading to tiny Loch Nant. It is pure delight.

Past Kilchrennan, with a plain and dignified church, a minor road to the left leads to Ardanaiseig. At the big house there is one of those wonderful gardens produced by the balmy climate of Scotland's west coast and by much skilled labour, love and money. Rhododendrons and azaleas in particular bloom and blossom there with a prolific freedom found nowhere else, not even in their native Himalayan homeland. Quite simply, Ardanaiseig is lovely, and the garden is open to the public. The paths lead through massed colour to the shores of Loch Awe and open views to high mountains across the water.

Back to the road running down Loch Awe. This is a very pleasant drive, with the Loch on one side of the road and wooded hills on the other.

Loch Awe, of course, is the longest freshwater loch in Scotland, twenty five miles from end to end, but barely a mile wide. Previously, before the bowdlerising cartographers got to work, it was Lochow and there is an old saying, long used by Scots far from home and in trouble: 'It's a far cry to Lochow'.

Before the days of metalled roads, it was used as a major highway, and in fact was the only means of access to the lands to the east. The number of castles on its shores and its islands attest to its importance as a means of communication. Even in prehistoric days it was important, and at least 20 crannogs have been located. These were prehistoric artificial islands built in the Loch, on which strong points were erected to which the people could retreat in times of strife and danger. The crannogs were reached by underwater tracks which twisted and turned in a way known only to the people of that area.

For much of the way, the road down the Loch runs through forests, but they are not the massed and serried ranks which desecrate so many Highland hills. Somehow, this is the accept able face of forestry, and it adds to the beauty of the countryside, rather than destroying it.

About 8 miles south from Kilchrenan, an even more minor road goes off up the hill away from Loch Awe, and leads to Loch Avich and eventually to the coast just south of Kilninver. This is a grand drive and very much worth doing. Even better is the walk by hill tracks from Duninveran on Loch Avich through the valley to Braglenbeg and roadhead at Scamadale. It is perfectly possible for the walkers to take that lonely track while the driver goes round by road to meet them. A great way to enjoy a half day. And the walkers will have trodden a track travelled through all of history and much of prehistory, for that is the 'String Of Lorne' road.

Loch Avich itself is legendary (and legends are the raw material of history) for on an island at the south west of the Loch there was the 'Castle of the Red-Haired Girl' of Fingalian legend.

More precisely, one version of the legend places it there.

But if you keep to the main road down Loch Awe, you come to Inverliever, at the foot of Glen Liever. There is an Adventure School there now, but whatever the young people do today, it cannot compare with what happened in 1499. This was a Campbell lairdship, of course, and the second Earl of Argyll sent the Laird and his seven sons to kidnap little Muriello Cawdor, heiress of the Thanes of Cawdor in Perthshire. The Earl, for no good reason, claimed she was his ward and wanted her married off to one of his sons.

All seven of the laird's sons were killed in the fight with Cawdor's men, but the Campbells prevailed. When she saw what was happening, the girl's mother branded the face of the four year old child with a red hot key and bit off a finger tip, in the hope that thus disfigured, the child would not be acceptable to the Earl. But it didn't work, and the child was carried off and married off, and eventually the Cawdor lands passed into the rapacious maw of the Campbells, which of course was the object of the exercise in the first place.

The village of Ford, at the head of Loch Awe, was originally the Ford of the Hazels. The hotel in the village was once a drovers' inn, in the days when cattle from the islands and Highlands were driven south over tracks still visible and walkable today. To arouse the envy of all anglers, the biggest salmon ever caught in Britain was taken at Ford. A whole 89 pounds. One wonders what tackle was used in that epic battle.

If for some reason you do not want to complete the journey down the west side of Loch Awe, then pause at Dalavich. This is a Forestry Commission village, and fits well enough into its environment of hills and water. There are no other communities of any size for many miles from Dalavich, and the Forestry Commission workers must be very self-sufficient people.

This is almost entirely Forestry Commission country, and it bears all the marks of it, with its miles of quick-growing conifers.

And yet it does not have the overbearing monotony that stamps others forests. There are many hardwood trees, glowing like torches in autumn colour against the darkness of the conifers, and viewpoints and forest trails have been carefully established and maintained. Since the Forestry Commission is freely damned for its many sins, at least let it be praised for its few virtues.

A few miles south of Dalavich village, in the Inverliever Forest, (which is the oldest State Forest in Scotland, having been bought in 1907) is Kilmaho, and at Fiddler's Point there, projecting into the loch, is a very ancient chapel. It is a bit difficult to reach, being sadly overgrown, but well worth the effort. The chapel is that of St. Mochoe, of the late 5th cent. Although much damaged by a great gale in 1968, there are still two oval ruins, and nearby two cross-slabs. An outcrop of rock is carved with a Maltese Cross and some small cloaked figures with bird heads. Those heads mean that they go right back to the ancient Picts and their little-understood beliefs.

Quite close is what the maps call 'New York', but don't expect some sort of high rise metropolis. There is nothing but a ruined house and a decrepit pier. It got its name from the York Building Co., a name still remembered and loathed in the Highlands. That company bought up many Highland estates, and anything else easily moveable, after the confiscations which followed the 1745 rising. They looted what they could from the properties they had bought, and then went bankrupt, conveniently, and to no-one's sorrow.

Loch Avich is close by, and the hill road from the B845 on Loch Awe over to the main A816 past Kilmelford is a road of great delight, whichever way you travel it. It is no highway, though, and some care is needed. The loch itself is deep in the hills, and lonely but beautiful. Once it was known as Loch Luina, and there is an ancient saga called *CoMluina* or the Conflict at Luina. At the western end of the loch the very few ruins of a very old castle stand on a tiny island. This is *Caisteal-n'-Ighinneruaiddh*, the Castle of the Red Headed Girl, and is another relic of the great Fingalian days.

From Loch Avich House, a very slight track strikes out even deeper into the hills to Loch Scammadale and finally down to the main road at Glen Eurchar, just south of Kilninver on the A816. That is the track for you if you really want loneliness. It is the 'String of Lorne' road, once the only highway through these mountain vastnesses, and it was on that lonely road that Sir Colin Campbell was slain by a MacDougall ambush in 1294. A cairn, *Cairn Chailean*, marks the spot, just to the left of the track immediately past tiny Loch na Sreinge. Sir Colin's castle still stands on a tiny islet in Loch Awe, just opposite Dalavich.

It was Sir Colin's son, Sir Neil, the first Mac Cailean Mor, who gave such invaluable support to Robert Bruce during the Wars of Independence and who, after victory, was rewarded with grants of land which led finally to the Campbell hegemony over much of Argyll. Sir Colin, Cailean Mor, has a memorial in Kilchrenan kirkyard, on the shore of Loch Awe, a kirkyard well worth visiting for its wealth of carved stones of great age. His original tombstone is built into the east gable of the church.

LOCH AWE--SOUTH SIDE

A circuit of Loch Awe would assuredly make a remarkable day out. There is hardly a mile without some interesting relic of the past, and certainly not a mile without a memorable view.

The road down the north side of the loch has been described already, as far as Ford, and from Ford another road keeps to the south side of the loch. Be sure the loch is on your left! About three miles from the hotel at Ford there are the ruins of Finchurn Castle. There is not much of it left today, but you can see that it was a small square building with tiny rooms opening off the central hall. It has long been in ruins, but its end was interesting.

Long ago, before the rise of Campbell power in the area, the local laird was insistent that all the rights and privileges of his chief-hood should be followed. There was a young girl, daughter of a vassal, and her wedding day had come. She was to be married to the young man she loved. But the chief had let it be known that he intended to exercise his alleged feudal right, and to spend the night of the wedding with young Una.

After the wedding ceremony, the party, including the chief, sat down to feast in the house of Una's father. But the bridegroom was missing. A search party was sent out, and they returned very shortly to cry that Finchurn Castle was ablaze.

Even for a chief with other things on his mind, it was clear what had happened. The chief rushed out to seek the bridegroom-culprit. But the young man was ready for him, and they met face to face in a wood. The conflict was short and bitter, but the chief fell, fatally wounded, and no doubt had time to reflect, before he died, that the night had not turned out quite as he had expected.

Just by the ruins of Finchurn, a footpath leads south all the way to Loch Fyne. This, too, was a drove road, and it passes close by the original church of Glassary. Glassary was a very important church and parish long ago, and the ruined church, roofless and stark, bears this out. It is said that the church was built with stone quarried at Crarae on Loch Fyne, where there are great quarries to this day, and that the stones were passed hand to hand all the ten long miles to the building site.

If you look closely at the stone by the nave door, you should just discern the Devil's handprint. The legend is that one night a tailor was working by the door (I can't imagine why) when the Devil appeared and demanded his soul. The tailor refused, and with a cry of 'I see that, but I sew this' nailed the Devil's hand to the stones with his bodkin.

Be that as it may, the churchyard has many very interesting and very ancient carved stones. A grand place indeed to pass an hour.

Continuing on the Loch Awe road, you soon come to Portinisherrich, with the tiny islet of *Eilean an-t Sagort,* or Priest's Island, just off shore. This was a burial place in olden days, and the ruined chapel of the custodian can still be seen on the lochside. There are many such island burial places in the Highlands, and a visit to them is a pilgrimage, really. They are fine and quiet places, unkempt and overgrown, and you stumble over fallen stones which once marked the graves of chiefs and warriors, once important people before whom the world trembled, but who now lie mouldered and forgotten.

On another small off-shore island at Port Innisherrich are the ruins of Innischonnell Castle. It was in that castle, ruined and desolate now, that Donal Dubh -- Black Donald -- was held as an infant. He was the child of Angus of Islay, and had a valid claim to the Lordship of the Isles. He was kidnapped by the Earl of Atholl and handed over to the Earl of Argyll, who may have been his grandfather and who certainly did not want another claimant to the Lordship. This all happened in 1480, but it is still spoken of as though it were yesterday. Black Donald was held a prisoner until 1501, then released during a raid by the MacDonalds of Glencoe. He led a rebellion of the island chiefs to claim his Lordship, but it failed and he was imprisoned in Edinburgh in 1506. That really ended the Lordship of the Isles, and indeed ended a very long chapter of Scottish history.

LOCH ETIVE

It is impossible to see much of Loch Etive from the road or from any vehicle, and that is good. Some places should remain secret, and only give up their secrets to those prepared to work for the privilege. Loch Etive, surely, is one such place.

Yet you can drive to the head of Loch Etive on a fairly rough but adequate road from the A82, just north of Kingshouse (that is, on

ROE DEER

the road through Glencoe). It is a lovely road, even though you must drive back the ten miles from the head of the loch. The road follows the course of the river at first, as it twists and turns and leaps from pool to pool between great bare hillsides through the Royal Forest. At Dalness, halfway along the road, the narrow glen opens out to become a placid valley. The river turns there, from west to south-west.

There is a grassy slope just across the river at Dalness, and it was there that Deirdre and Naoise had their 'grianan' or sunny bower. This happened when the world was young and lovely, when everything was innocent, and only the hearts of men were black.

Deirdre was the most beautiful of women. So beautiful was she that all men and all beasts gave her their adoration. She loved Naoise, the most handsome of men, and the two lived their idyll together, at the grianan on that grassy slope, where fruit trees flourished.

But the beauty of Deirdre was such that it brought evil into the minds of men. As the two young lovers, supremely happy, roamed the hills and passed their days in gladness, King Conchobar in distant Ireland, distraught with his passion for Deirdre, sent emissaries to bring the two lovers to him.

They were playing draughts one day in the grianan when a great shout echoed up the glen, disturbing the red deer and startling the eagle from his roost on the peaks. Deirdre knew that the great shout came from the throat of Fergus, emissary of Conchobar, for she had the gift of second sight, as well as the curse of unparalleled beauty. She persuaded Naoise that it was the voice of one who lived in the glen. Again came the great shout, and again the red deer lifted their heads from the sweet grass, and again Deirdre persuaded her lover that there was no stranger in the glen. And again it came, and this time Naoise could not be persuaded, for he knew this must be Fergus, Knight of the Red Branch.

So Naoise sent his brother to welcome Fergus and a feast was prepared. And during that feast Fergus persuaded Deirdre and Naoise to travel with him to Ireland, promising them safety and wealth. Deirdre knew better, and as they sailed down Loch Etive in Fergus's galley 'Iubhrach', she sang her farewell to Scotland, a haunting song of infinite sadness that we know today, and which still moves to tears.

She was right, of course. King Conchobar had Naoise killed and claimed the lovely, sorrowful Deirdre. But whatever joys he gained from his evil, they did not last, for Deirdre died. We remember her for her beauty and by the infinite pathos of her song: we remember him only for his treachery, and we remember that with execration.

There is a goddess of Loch Etive and of the Glen. It is not Deirdre, for she has long gone. The goddess is Eiteah, and she used to come swirling in the mist and rain and sudden howling winds down from the high tops and swoop down the Loch, endangering the galleys and the little fishing boats that once thronged these waters. We hear little of her these days, or perhaps it is simply that the Children of the Mist have gone now, leaving a sad and lovely emptiness, and there is no one to tell of Eiteah. Nor of Deirdre.

But back to the road. If you have reached the head of Loch Etive, surely you will want to walk a little and linger over the views, for they are splendid. You do have to return the way you came, but in some ways the hills and the glen are even better as you go back to the main road through Glen Coe and on to the north. Perhaps it is that a little of Deirdre still lingers by that grianan, and that she touches all who think of her.

Surely one of the grandest walks in all the Highlands is that 20 mile-long track running from Kinlochetive, where the road ends, south and east to Loch Tulla, near to the main A82 road through Glencoe. It can be started at Loch Tulla, which is reached by following the spur of road (it is actually the old Glencoe road) running left to Loch Tulla by Bridge of Orchy. From road-head there, the walkers go west and south, past Loch Dochart and through Glen Kinglas to the shores of Loch Etive, then north to Kinlochetive, where, if organisation is good, the vehicle can be waiting.

It is a supremely fine walk through Scotland's grandest scenery. You are far enough from the mountains to see them properly, not foreshortened by being close, and you will see them in all their grandeur.

Of course, you can see a good deal of Loch Etive, but not the Glen, from both the north and the south sides at the foot of the Loch. The road from Dalmally to Oban (A85) runs along the southern shore for a while, and if you are travelling south on A828 from Fort William to Oban, there is a grand minor road, B845, which takes you to the northern shore. It turns off the main road at Barcaldine and is a splendid trip with majestic views of mountain and sea.

CRINAN AND DISTRICT

South of Oban, heading for Lochgilphead and Kintyre, is one of the most fascinating districts in the whole of Britain.

For one thing, there is Dunadd. This, more than any other place in the whole vast area represents ancient days and ancient ways. Dunadd Castle, on the river Add, just a few miles north of Lochgilphead on the main A817 by Kilmichael Glassary, is one of the oldest known inhabited sites in Scotland, and can lay fair claim to being the very womb of the nation.

There is nothing much to see now, just a ruckle of stones, a few low walls and a filled-in well. But there is a wild boar easily and fluently outlined on a rock outcrop, and close to it a hollowed water container and a footprint. No-one, and certainly no Scot, can look at these and be unmoved. Let me tell you about it.

Dunadd stands at the very top of a steep rock outcrop, 176 feet high, in the midst of a great moss or peat bog. Stand there, and immediately you can see the strategic value of this place. Today, the plain is sprinkled with farms and trees: fifteen hundred years ago it must have been a desolation over which no enemy could approach unseen. The views are quite spectacular and must have been so even then, with the great forests of Knapdale, the peak of Ben Cruachan, the Paps of Jura and even Corrievrechan in full view. Below, the river Add winds in from Loch Crinan, and provided easy passage for boats. There is a good and easy pass over the mountains through Kilmartin Glen and Loch Awe, and thence to central Scotland, or up the west coast to the Great Glen and the plains of the north-east. The flat valley through which the Crinan Canal now runs provided easy and safe access to what is now Lochgilphead and so on to Loch Fyne and the Clyde Coast and down sheltered waters to Ireland. A natural stronghold indeed, and one used as such from the Stone Age onwards.

Over the centuries, Dunadd became an elaborate centre, protected by more than seventy other forts within a ten mile radius. No area of Scotland is more rich in relics of the long past.

Dunadd moves out of the mists of pre-history when the three brothers Fergus, Lorne and Angus sailed from Ireland, up the Add, and fortified Dunadd in AD 503. Perhaps they had to fight for it, for certainly it had been a fort for many centuries before that. However, it became the seat of Fergus. He had brought with him the Stone of Destiny, *Lia Fail*, which had long been used as the coronation seat for Kings of Ireland. Tradition and belief held that this was the very stone used as a pillow by Jacob at Bethel, and for centuries it had been preserved at Cashel Cathedral.

The Stone of Destiny was used as a coronation seat by Fergus, and all subsequent Scottish kings until it was seized by the English in 1296 and transported to Westminster Abbey, and used then by the English kings. In the Act of Union between England and Scotland it was laid down that the Stone of Destiny would be returned to Scotland, but that was never done.

You may recall that some few years ago it was removed from Westminster by Scots patriots and brought back to Scotland, leading to a farcical cops and robbers episode that Compton Mackenzie could have used as a sequel to Whisky Galore. Eventually, the Stone of Destiny, or something rather like it, was recovered and replaced under the Coronation Throne in Westminster Abbey.

It is not an impressive thing of itself, being merely a roughish block of red sandstone, measuring 26ins. by 16 3/4ins. by 10 1/2ins., but it has a tremendous symbolism.

The Stone of Destiny itself, and the carved water container or laver, the carving of the boar and the footprint, are all symbols of kingship, and were all used in coronation ceremonies at Dunadd until in 843 Kenneth MacAlpin moved his seat to Scone in Perthshire, a more central place for a more centralised Kingdom. The Stone of Destiny, indeed, is often referred to as the Stone of Scone.

Dunadd was the capital of Dalriada, and the original Dalriada was in Ireland, from whence came Fergus to found the Dalriadic Kingdom in Scotland. That was not the beginning of it though, for Dalriada in Ireland was founded by *Cruithne* (corn eaters: it was the Romans who called them Picts) from Alba, or Scotland. They stayed and prospered for generations in Ireland before the tide reversed, and now calling themselves Scots, returned to Dunadd to found the Scottish Dalriada. All a bit confusing perhaps, especially when you work it out that Ireland was founded by Scots and Scotland by the Irish!

The first movement of Scots from the Irish Dalriada into Scotland came about 230 AD, but it was comparatively small, and the Picts, who occupied the land, were too busy harrassing the Romans to pay much attention. The big movement of Scots came much later, when King Erc of Dalriada died in Antrim. Under the law of the Scots, the brother of Erc became King, and Erc's three sons, Fergus, Angus and Lorne, decided to leave their homeland and seek lordships in Alba -- Scotland. They arrived at Dunadd around A.D 503, with many followers, and determined on conquest.

Lorne went north, to the district which still bears his name. Angus took the off-shore islands, notably Islay, which was to be the main seat and power base of Kings and Lords of the Isles for almost a thousand years. Fergus took Kintyre, Knapdale and Cowal. He survived his brothers, and, again under the laws of the Scots, fell heir to their lands.

The King of Dalriada, Kenneth MacAlpin, finally battled and broke the Picts in 843, and Scotland was born, as Alba and Dalriada both faded away.

You have to use your imagination to visualise Dunadd as it was 1500 years ago. Almost certainly the top of the hill, approached through a rock gully, was roofed and used for ceremonial purposes, such as coronations. Lower down there are defensive positions joined by stone walls and even the very topmost keep had separate defensive positions. In those days, one supposes, there would be a clutter of huts surrounding the hillock and certainly many artifacts -- querns, pottery and tools have been found round about.

There is no full account yet available of all the archeological wonders to be found in this small area between Loch Awe and Loch Crinan. There is such a wealth of material that days, weeks, even, could be spent just looking at them. None, though, can be so moving as the simple rock carvings at the top of Dunadd hill. Those carvings, the circular laver, the footprint and the wild boar, take us directly back to the days when Scotland was struggling to be born.

From Dunadd, the short trip to Stockavullin, just south of Kilmartin on A816, is the best introduction to the wealth of remains in the area. There are so many monuments to pre-history hereabouts that Stonehenge seems insignificant. And you will probably have them all to yourself -- not being regulated and guided and guarded as at Stonehenge today.

The South Cairn at Nether Largie is from perhaps 3000 B.C., and is one of the largest in Britain, being about 135 feet in diameter. Inside, the funeral chamber is 19 feet long, roofed by great slabs and floored with clean gravel. It is reached by a tunnel from the side. It seems that this burial cairn was used over a long period, for many different types of burial were distinguished, with many bones, beakers and urns. Some of the bodies had been cremated and the bones and ashes put into urns. At other periods, stone coffins were built, with the bodies in a crouching position.

Many of the stones around Largie bear the mysterious cup-and-ring marks, whose significance no one now knows, although they do seem to be connected, in Western Europe, with the great and ancient religion of the Druids.

Near Nether Largie is the Templewood Stone Circle, dating from about 1600 B.C. There are eight standing stones in a circle, with a central monolith and a burial cairn.

The whole area around Kilmartin and the river is festooned

with an unbelievable wealth of chiefly Bronze Age relics.

Kilmartin village, with its castle and church, is interesting -- the church much more than the castle. Indeed, the main interest of the castle is the legend that an attempt was made there to murder Colin Campbell, but it was somehow foiled, and Colin made his way to safety through a burning outbuilding. But he was not safe then, because the flames made his armour so hot that he had to jump into the river to cool off, and almost drowned before being rescued.

The church itself is not old, having been built only in 1835 on the site of an older church. It is the kirkyard and its stones you will want to see, for the two Kilmartin Crosses are there.

On the right hand side, just inside the gateway, is one cross showing Christ crucified on one side and Christ in majesty on the other. It dates probably from the 10th cent. Opposite is a lovely Celtic Cross, probably 12th cent., of greenish slate with traditional Celtic carving.

Those are not the only items of interest at Kilmartin. There is a collection of gravestones of the Malcolm chiefs. These are very fine indeed, with carved knights in armour and other devices. Most impressive of all, surely, is the enclosure (now glass roofed) inscribed '*Heir lyes Master Neil Campbell and Christiane Campbell 1627*'. Neil Campbell was Bishop of Argyll and the Isles in the late 16th cent., and in the burial enclosure with him there has been collected a wonderful mixture of early medieval work, tomb stones, slabs and memorials, many of them with the typical West Highland decorations of swords and crosses. On one is a fullsize knight in armour. The whole kirkyard is a treasure house of the past, and well repays a close examination.

Kilmartin Castle, at the north end of the village, is ruined and neglected, but can still be seen as a 16th cent. fortalice, and a large one. It was built by John Carswell, who preceded Neil Campbell as Bishop of Argyll and the Isles. In fact, when he became Bishop, he left Kilmartin Castle and, as befitted his new dignity and wealth, built a larger castle nearby at Carnassarie.

He was a man of some fame and many weaknesses, but is best remembered as being the instigator of the first book to be printed in Gaelic, a translation of the Liturgy of John Knox, published in 1567. It is perhaps significant that there is a still-remembered Gaelic rhyme about Carsewell:-

At Corselach Mor in Carnasserie
There are five quarters in his house.
His rump is like the back of a crane.
His stomach empty, greedy, and unfortunately
capacious.

In any case, his new castle at Carnasserie is large and impressive. It stands a mile further north, and is a splendid place. It is not, of course, so very old as things go in this district, dating only from about 1522, but it was deliberately built in an archaic style. There is a tall keep and two wings, very elaborately worked and carved, and an unnecessary display of gun-ports and shot-holes. An archway into a courtyard carries the date 1685 and the initials of the Campbells, for naturally that family took possession of Carnassarie, as they did with everything else that was not positively nailed down.

South west of Kilmartin, on the little headland between Loch Crinan and the Sound of Jura, is Poltalloch House and Duntroon Castle, both well worthy of a visit. The mansion house, sadly, is roofless and abandoned, but the nearby Episcopalian Church of St. Columba and the kirkyard contain some very interesting and ancient stones. There is a delightful, though badly eroded, carving of a bishop over the entrance door. The Cross of Argyll, or the Archibald's Cross, is here, and that dates from 1355. It is a lovely slender crucifix with Christ on one side and very beautiful Celtic interlaced carving on the other. Even older, there is a prehistoric burial-chamber just to the west of the church.

Duntroon Castle is lovely, beautifully placed on a little headland and dating from the 13th cent. (although with some later additions). There was no attempt to level the site before building, and the structure flows gracefully round the rock contours, seeming to grow out of the solid rock. It has been well and thoughtfully restored now, and is a fine example of a Highland castle. Originally built as a curtain-walled structure with a keep, the 16th cent. additions made it into an 'L' shaped tower house. There are fine vaulted basements and many rooms and chambers actually within the thickness of the walls. Originally, the curtain walls would have enclosed some sort of hall, probably of wood, and a whole mass of minor buildings and dwellings, really a small town in itself.

It was a Campbell stronghold, of course, although the Malcolms took it over in 1792. It was besieged in 1644, during the Montrose wars, and a ghostly piper haunted the place after that -- one of Colkitto's, pipers, killed in the assault. He is not there now, for he finally found his peace just a few years ago when an Episcopalian minister used one of the basements as his chapel, and finding himself and his congregation sadly disturbed by the ghostly piper, exorcised him at last.

This whole area is so full of ancient monuments that a full description would be tedious -- perhaps impossible. But it is well worth the exploring, if only to realise how long man has lived and flourished here, even from long before Fergus MacErc arrived at Dunadd.

Perhaps if you wish for real quietness and loneliness in this whole quiet area, you are most likely to find it in the Tayvallich peninsula, on Danna Island and on the east side of Loch Sween.

Both sides of Loch Sween well repay exploration. Turn off the main A816 Oban-Lochgilphead road on to B841 at Cairnbaan, about four miles north of Lochgilphead and travel along the Crinan Canal (itself very interesting) to Bellanoch, where B8025 joins on the left. Take that road south through Knapdale Forest on the narrow tongue of land between Loch Sween and the Sound of Jura. It is an area badly served by roads, and none the worse for that, but is of outstanding beauty and much historical and archeological interest. You have to return the same way, but that is no hardship when the countryside is so attractive, and there is so much to look at and enjoy.

The enveloping forests of Knapdale have hidden and made inaccessible many historical sites, but sad though that might be, there are lots of others readily available. Perhaps, though, this area is best enjoyed just for its scenic beauty and quietness.

Apart from the scenery, the major attraction must be Castle Sween, about two-thirds of the way down the east side of the Loch. This astonishing ruin is claimed to be the oldest stone castle in all of Scotland, that land of multitudinous stone castles. Dating in the main from the 12th cent., there is a great curtain wall enclosing a courtyard seventy feet by fifty feet. There is a keep and towers at the corners, each pierced by arrow-slits, and a defensive parapet walk round the curtain walls. The south-west corner is broken down, the result of an attack by Colkitto, the lieutenant of Montrose, who seems to have successfully attacked half the castles in Scotland. That was in 1648. Much earlier -- four hundred years earlier -- Robert Bruce captured the castle, not once, but twice.

The name 'Sween ' is said to derive from the Norse 'Suibhne,' from a Prince of that name, Suibhne ma Righ Lochlann, son of the King of Norway, but in fact he died before the the castle was built. Conceivably, it was built on the site of an earlier fort.

Castle Sween used to be known as 'The Key Of Knapdale', and one can see why. King Robert Bruce besieged and took the castle, and captured the Lord of the Isles there. The King made Angus Og, another MacDonald, the new Lord of the Isles, and so valiant was the conduct of Angus and his men at Bannockburn that they were granted the privilege of always fighting on the King's right hand in every battle.

That was a great distinction and honour, and one that the MacDonalds cherished. They were denied that right at Culloden, and did not participate there as fully and valiantly as was their wont. Perhaps that terminal battle of the Highlanders would have gone differently had not Prince Charles Edward, typically, decided to impose his own ideas on the battleformation, and in doing so offended his staunchest allies.

Castle Sween continued to dominate everything around it until 1644, when it was attacked and sacked by Col Ciotach, Sir Alexander MacDonald. Today a ruin, it is still most impressive.

Further south again is Kilmory and the ruins of the 13th cent. Knap Chapel of St. Maelrubha. This has been converted into a museum for a very fine collection of carved stones, including the especially fine McMillan's Cross. This stands eight feet high on a plinth, with Christ crucified on one side and a vivid scene of deer, hounds and huntsmen on the other -- a rather strange combination. It dates from the 15th cent. There are perhaps thirty medieval grave slabs in the collection, and very fine they are. One shows the sort of large shears used by weavers for cutting cloth, and this might well indicate that Kilmory was once the site of a cloth industry. Certainly there has been a very long tradition of hand-weaving here, a tradition very recently ended.

There is a prayer stone there, too. This is a stone ball set in a cupped stone, and after praying, one was meant to turn the ball *deiseal* or sun-wise. That made the prayers more effective. Whilst wondering what would have happened had the stone ball been turned against the sun, it is worth also pondering that this practice of using the turning of a stone ball in prayer is quite similar to the practice of using the Tibetan prayer-wheel.

This area was the scene of one the battles of the Crofters' War of last century, when an alien landowner sought to evict his tenants. There was a whole village there, Stronfield, and prosperous enough it was. But the proprietor wanted the people out, and he sent his gamekeepers and some police to evict them. The crofters fought back, and the laird's men retired beaten. But more police were called in and the houses burned and the people evicted, to live or die as best they might. You can still see the ruined houses, a desolation and a sadness in that land of beauty.

A foot-track runs from the end of the road at Kilmory over to Loch Caolisport at Ellery. Ellery itself is at the end of a minor road

OTTERS

which joins B8024 running down the west side of Knapdale, and eventually to Tarbert. If you take that minor road, or walk the foot-track from Kilmory, you will find St. Columba's Cave. Coming by road, it is easy to miss this. There are some ruins, an old chapel, just after leaving Achahoish, but you pass these and go to the end of the road, another two miles. There you will find the cave, behind some medieval remains.

I suppose it is not quite certain that it was really St. Columba himself who stayed there and served Mass, but the tradition is unquestionably very strong. In any case, some man of God certainly stayed there during the Dark Ages. In the cave there is an altar with a cross carved above it and a basin for the Holy Water. It is a place haunted by the past, and in some ways reminiscent of Iona, where no-one can fail to be moved by the

simplicity and the sheer human courage of those who brought word of a new god to a heathen people well satisfied with their own beliefs.

But back now to the road junction and down the Tayvallich Peninsula. 'Tayvallich', incidentally, is properly *Tigh-na-Bhea laich* -- the House of the Pass.

There are several forest walks well marked on this road, and taking them ensures some fine views of the Hebrides. Just by Tayvallich itself is a grand beach of golden sand, and it would be difficult to think of anywhere better to spend a lazy day. It faces out over the Sound of Jura, to Jura itself, and the views of those lovely hills are magnificent. Continuing south beyond Tayvallich, with good views at every twist of the road, one comes finally to another road junction. For the moment, stay with the main road to Keills. Just north of the road, there is a ruined 13th cent. chapel, with yet another well-renowned collection of carved stones. Amongst them is the tombstone of Ewen Buchach Lorne, John MacDonald of Lorn, who was the foe of both Wallace and Bruce, and was English King Edward's Admiral of the Western Seas. Also look for the ancient carving of the Celtic harp, with every string shown. There is a fine Celtic Cross, too, and at Keilmore, beside the ruined chapel, is another excellent Celtic cross, with a most curious set of carvings. There seems to be an angel looking down into a bird's nest with three eggs. There are two otters and two dogs and a cloaked figure and some fine Celtic tracery. Who knows what that artist of remote antiquity had in mind when he cut at the stone? It is a puzzle with no answer.

In the burial ground near the chapel are many recumbent stones, and one of them, marking the grave of a Graham of Claverhouse, has a small hole pierced at the head, so that he who rests below can look up and through the chapel window to the wild country beyond, which he loved so well.

If you take the minor road over the causeway to Danna Island you will be rewarded with spectacular Hebridean views. And you

CRINAN BASIN

will know that you have come to the end of the road. You must return the way you came, all the way to Crinan, but surely you will not begrudge one mile of a fascinating journey.

It is difficult to say which is more delightful, running south down Loch Sween to the open sea, or travelling back along the road towards all the hills and glens of central Argyll. In any case, you have them both, for return almost to Crinan you must. The eastern shore of the Loch would, by no more than a whisker, have my vote for its scenic splendours. And perhaps also for its particular jewelled beauty, for on that shore there is a great wealth of wild flowers, which do not flourish amongst the bracken and heather of the western shore.

Travelling south to Knapdale and Kintyre, you must at some point cross the Crinan Canal. You can see Loch Crinan and the canal from the top of Dunadd Castle, itself now a quiet ruin after being once the the heart of Scotland. Not so long ago, the Canal was a vital waterway, and a busy one too, but now it is left to the pleasure boats, and one wonders for how much longer.

A canal across that great peninsula was an obvious necessity in the days when most transport in the Highlands was sea borne and when great fleets of sailing boats fished these waters. The voyage round the Mull of Kintyre was long and arduous -- a canal would save time and lives. So, around 1800 it was decided to build a canal.

James Watt, one of those polymaths that the Industrial Revolution produced, surveyed the area and recommended two possibilities, one at West Loch Tarbert and the other at Crinan. Rather oddly, the latter was chosen. It was not an easy canal to build, and more than once the swampy banks collapsed. After 18 years of effort Thomas Telford was brought in to finish the work, and the government gave some financial support. It was finished eventually, and was immediately very busy.

It was not the easiest canal to build, nor was it the easiest to operate. The locks are so close together that passengers were always encouraged to walk most of the canal length rather than wait for the boat's passage.

Today, for most of the year it lies still, except for an occasional fishing boat. During the summer months it is busy enough with pleasure craft of all kinds.

A road, B841, runs almost its full length, from Crinan to Lochgilphead, and it is interesting. Not so interesting, though, as in the days when the canal was busy with trade, fishing boats and passengers. At first, there was a horse-drawn barge for passengers, pulled by three horses, and with postillions in full livery. Queen Victoria herself travelled on that barge during her majestic tour of the Highlands in 1847, but was definitely not amused when there was an hour's delay en route, which she found 'tedious'. Then there was a strange steam barge, the *Linnet,* which was said to resemble a tram car floating up the canal.

But the developing of the road network, and lorries and buses has killed all that. It has even killed off the old steam-puffers, which, not so long ago, plied to every village and beach in the Highlands and Islands, and used the Crinan Canal as their main highway from Glasgow to the Islands and the West Coast.

The whole area round Crinan is rich in mementoes and memorials of the past. There is Dunadd, of course, where Scotland's story first began. Kilmartin and Kilmichael Glassary are both nearby, and both have remarkable collections of old carvings. Indeed, you can hardly step on soil here that does not bear some relic or memory of olden days.

At Kilmichael, just above the churchyard with its great wealth of sculptured stones, there is a great flat rock covered with those mysterious cup-and-ring marks whose purpose no one now knows. More interesting are two small footprints carved into the rock and facing north-east, as does the one at Dunadd, where kings were crowned. It has been conjectured that these prints at Kilmichael mark the place where the queens of Dalriada were crowned. Old literature repeatedly stresses the importance of the Queens. Perhaps their importance was given formal recognition here at Kilmichael.

KINTYRE

Kintyre is almost an island. A neck of land less than one mile wide separates East and West Loch Tarbert, and at its highest point that neck of land is only 47 feet above sea level. From that narrow neck, the great peninsula, 40 miles long and 8 miles wide, probes south towards Ireland, only twelve miles away from the Mull. Kintyre is a quiet and lovely place, full of history and strange contrasts, beautiful and remote.

Not only is Kintyre almost an island, it has sometimes been treated as though it was in reality part of the Hebrides. King Magnus Barefoot of Norway laid claim to the Hebrides, and to prove that all the fertile lands of Kintyre were part of the Hebrides, had his boat, with himself at the helm, dragged across the narrow spit of land at the head of Loch Tarbert, thereby proving that he could circumnavigate Kintyre, which must therefore be an island! King Edgar of Scotland had agreed with that piece of legalistic casuistry, but in point of fact neither King controlled the area: the Scottish Lords of the Isles did that.

'*Kintyre* ' comes from the Gaelic *Ceann Tire* -- The Head Of the Land, and the Mull itself well justifies the name. There are great cliffs there, sheer and storm-battered, and tremendous swirling tides.

It was at this remote place that the first restless waves of humanity reached Scotland. Almost certainly those Mesolithic people, migratory hunters and fishers, came from northern Ireland, as did their successors, the Neolithic people and the Bronze Age people. The first immigrants of whom we have some knowledge, the Scots, certainly came from northern Ireland. There were three sons of Erc, from northern Ireland, who came to Scotland with their followers,

TARBERT

and one of them, Fergus, stayed in Kintyre and received that as his inheritance. Aidan, the great-grandson of Fergus, was crowned by St. Columba as king of the Scottish Dalriada in 574 (there was alrady a Dalriada in Ireland).

But for hundreds of years it was the Lords of the Isles who controlled Kintyre, ruling it as a fiefdom, paying little attention to the demands of the Scottish kings. Only as the power of those kings increased and the power of the State grew were they able to extend westwards. In the 17th cent. Kintyre was granted to the Earl of Argyll, and he subdued what resistance was left, eliminating most of the population in the process, and transplanted many Lowlanders there, chiefly Gaelic-speakers from Ayshire. Inevitably, you enter Kintyre from the north, by Tarbert.

This is a fine little town, very colourful, and with a busy harbour. Not so busy with fishing boats these days, but Tarbert is a favourite yachting centre, and the harbour is usually bright with small boats. It is an old town, and was made a burgh in 1328.

Bruce's Castle broods above the town, ivy-mantled and ancient. It was not built by Bruce, for it stood there since long before the 13th cent., but certainly he had it repaired and strengthened. Robert Bruce knew the area well, and wandered over much of Kintyre during his long years of adversity. There is a cave just north of Tarbert where tradition insists that the King lay one long winter's night, warmed and comforted by a goat which shared his vigil, and whose milk he drank. He did not forget, and when he was king in both word and deed, he enacted a law forbidding anyone to impound a goat. He revisited Tarbert, and ordered that a road be built between Tarbert and West Loch Tarbert, and himself paid £13:16:8 for the cost.

Like so many other places on the west of Scotland, Tarbert was long dependent on the herring, that fickle fish which no longer visits those shores in the great shoals of old. Indeed, it is claimed that their breeding grounds have been destroyed by trawling, and that never again will those shoals appear. But there is still some fishing

from Tarbert, even if you cannot now walk dry shod across the harbour, stepping from boat to boat, as was possible not so long ago.

As an introduction to a lovely piece of country, Tarbert serves well. It is a fine, welcoming, couthy little place, and ideally situated for anyone wise enough to spend time in Kintyre.

When touring in Kintyre, there are no alternatives. You go south, then north again. The peninsula has a very rocky spine, and no roads cross it. There is one road following the east coast and one the west, and they only join at Campbeltown, far south. In the north, the east and west coast roads are joined together by the B8001, which leaves the main road about six miles south of Tarbert. Since you have to go south and return north, it is much better to travel south on the east coast. You will have the sun with you then.

Leave Tarbert, then, by the A83, running along the south shore of West Loch Tarbert, and at Kennacraig take the B8001, on the left. This is a single track road, and care is required. It goes up over the rocky spine of the Kintyre peninsula, and falls to the sea again, to Kilbrannan Sound between Arran and Kintyre.

If the day is clear -- and they frequently are -- stop at the peak of the road and take time to look at the magnificent view. Off to the east lies Arran, with its fells and peaks clear-edged and hard, sometimes seeming so close that you could almost touch them. Below is Kilbrannan Sound, edged with white and golden sand, and with the velvet waters deep blue and light green. Off to the west are Islay and the mountains of Jura. Indeed, it is a sight to be savoured; a sight to lighten the heart.

As you approach the sea, by the ferry terminal for Arran, turn left up the dead-end road for Skipness. This is heading north, and you want to go south, but the diversion is supremely worth while. It is a strange little road, often covered in drifting sand from the shore, and winding between peculiar windworn rocks. Skipness village is entrancing, with a loud little stream dancing down the Glen and emptying into Kilbrannan Sound. Skipness was a Norse setlement -- the name means Ship Point -- but when Somerled, Lord of the Isles,

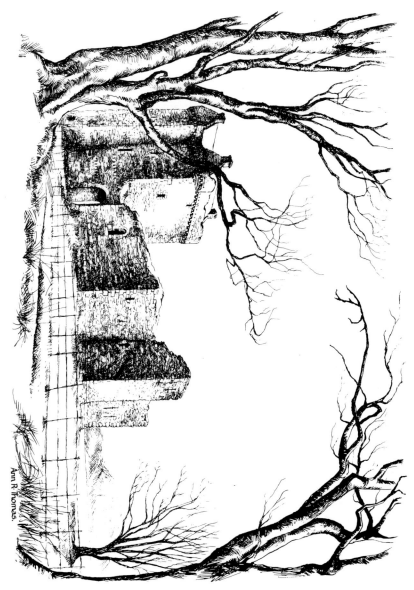

SKIPNESS CASTLE

broke the Norse power, the village became a peaceful settlement, and remains so to this day.

But the glory of Skipness is the ruined castle and chapel. A glance at a map shows how important and strategic Skipness must have been in the days when all transport was by sea. It dominates both the Sound of Kilbrannan and the Sound of Bute. It could control all shipping up Loch Fyne. The castle was built early in the 13th cent., and was at least twice strengthened and enlarged. Today the tower stands five stories high, facing out over the seas it once dominated. There is a kind of residual splendour about this ruin, and a peacefulness enhanced by the avenue of ancient trees by which one approaches.

We know that in 1246 a certain Dugfallas, son of Syfyn, lived there, and since those distant days, it has been occupied by MacDonalds, Macsweens, Stewarts and Campbells. It came into Campbell ownership in 1499 and with the Campbells came a fairy woman, a *glaistaig,* a little lady with long golden hair, wearing a green silk dress. She was a sort of family guardian, a kindly sprite who helped with all the housework after dusk, and who also warned the household if the Campbells were returning to the castle after an absence.

It is a big castle, of the Norman style, with a great wall, strengthened by three towers and a strong keep. It stands on a raised beach, and is built of local stone, except for red sandstone lintels, which must have been brought over from Arran.

Although it changed ownership so often, it was never taken, perhaps because of its very size (forty yards by thirty yards) and the obvious strength of its walls. Unusually for Scottish castles, it is not built on a rocky hill or outcrop, and is easily approached over level land. One would almost think that the builders had anticipat ed that it would never be attacked, and thus did not need the extra defence of a steep hill.

From the castle, a short walk takes you to the chapel, a fine 13th cent. structure, still impressive in its ruined state. It is dedicated

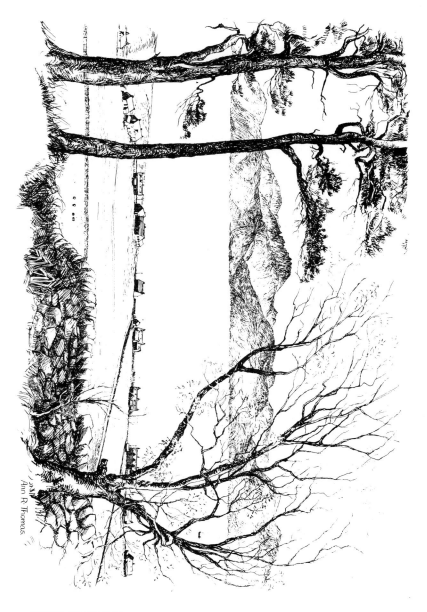

ARRAN FROM SKIPNESS

-111-

to St. Brendan, and there are some burial slabs there, and some grand headstones. One burial slab depicts a man armed with a spear and a sword, and wearing a conical helmet. Such mediaeval slabs, with their graphic carvings, tell us much about life in those dark days when the skills of writing had been lost to the mass of people, and were preserved only in the monasteries.

Back, then, to Skipness and on to the road south. It is a grand and twisting road, climbing and falling, always within sight and sound of the sea, and always with Arran's exciting hills fret-worked across the narrow sound.

If you are seeking delightful little bays of silver sand, they are here in plenty: if you want to stretch, then wander up a sheep track to the hills and hidden glens. And it would be difficult to imagine a more satisfying place for beach-combing than Cour Bay.

At Barmalloch the road leaves the coast and corkscrews its way up into Carradale Forest. A side road here, on the right, wanders off into the quiet hills, running alongside Carradale Water, and ending on the slopes of Deuchoran Hill. It is very much worth while climbing from the end of the road to the summit of the hill. It isn't much over one thousand feet high, but the whole world is below you. Jura, Islay, and Gigha islands lie dreaming to the west. The whole long length of Kintyre's hills are to the south, and to the north, across the forest, are more hills, with the great Highland mountains in the far distance. Delectable.

The road continues, swooping down from the forest to the wooded glen of Carradale. This is a great delight, especially perhaps in the spring when the trees are fresh-leaved and the massed rhododendrons in flower. But it is lovely at any time of year.

Carradale village lies a little off the road, but should be visited. There is a neat little harbour, still used by fishing boats, and the grounds of Carradale House, open in the summer months, are delightful. Carradale Bay is a great sweep of empty sand, and on one arm of the bay, on a little rocky islet which you can reach dryshod when the tide is out, there are the remains of a vitrified fort.

WILD GOATS ON CARRADALE POINT

This is a good example of such circular forts, whose origins are still a mystery, although believed to date from the first century. This particular vitrified fort presents strong evidence that the vitrification was done deliberately to strengthen the walls, and make a solid construction out of loose rubble. It must have been a great leap forward in technology in those distant days before mortar and cement had been invented, and it is interesting that that great leap should have been taken by Iron Age people.

One can well imagine how the fertile mind of some person worked. Some pieces of silica-bearing stones had been vitrified and fused strongly together in one of their primitive furnaces. Eureka! Why not build walls of this rock and then fire them? It would be a great improvement on the old loosely piled stones. So a wall was built, with brushwood and probably peat stacked between the stones, and then, on a day when the wind blew fresh, it was fired, and eventually, when all was cool again, there was a solid wall of stones fused together -- a glassy wall, just as we can see today. It was only sense to build whole forts in that way. That ancient, evocative structure at Carradale shows the results quite clearly.

Even glass palaces weather and fall into ruin, but of the fifty or so vitrified forts in Scotland, this one at Carradale is perhaps the most accessible and well-preserved. There is another in Kintyre, near Clachan on the west coast, but it is not nearly so easy to find and visit.

South-west of Carradale is Kintyre's highest hill, *Beinn an Tuirc* -- The Hill of the Boar -- and it is quite easy to climb. On this hill was enacted another of the Fingalian tragedies which, if legend is accepted as truth, once filled all this land with much drama and a lot of sorrow. This, like the legend of Deirdre, is a tale of when the world was young. It comes from the nation of heroes who occupied Argyll in those days, led by Fionn Mac Camhal, or Fingal.

Diarmid was the young man's name, and he was a great hero, handsome and fleet of foot, skilful in the chase and courageous in battle, and loyal to his leader Fingal. Grainne was the young woman, beautiful and chaste as were all maidens in those happy days. She was to marry Fingal himself, and her father, King Carmac, was delighted. But one day she met Diarmid in Fingal's train, and fell helplessly (and of course hopelessly) in love with him. She begged him to run away with her, but, loyal to his chief, and indeed loving his chief, Diarmid refused.

To remove himself from temptation, Diarmid took himself off from the halls of Fingal, and wandered the hills of Kintyre. The marriage of Grainne and Fingal took place, but, crazed by her love for Diarmid, Grainne also wandered into the hills and found her love. Fingal himself, and his men, believed that Diarmid was dead, but one day when hunting in the hills they found signs of him, and Fingal gave his great hunting cry, well knowing that Diarmid must reply. Grainne, too, was there, and they heard the cry. Grainne begged

Diarmid not to reply, but, when the great shout came again, he answered it, for he knew he had nothing to fear. Had he not always treated Grainne as his sister and the wife of his chief? Soon he was in the midst of the rejoicing band, and Grainne, heartbroken, stayed in the woods.

Fingal himself knew that his well-loved and lovely Grainne had been with Diarmid, but he did not speak of it. Instead they spoke of a great boar that Fingal had chased unsuccessfully, and he challenged Diarmid to kill that boar. The next day, after feasting, Diarmid set out to find the boar, and did so, on the slopes of the hill above Carradale. It was an epic encounter, but eventually the massive boar was killed, although in its maddened rush it had bent Diarmid's great sword like a reed.

When Fingal and his men came up, they saw the great boar dead, and Fingal asked Diarmid to measure it, for no such boar had been seen before. Diarmid paced out the animal from snout to tail, and called out that it was sixteen feet long. Fingal, who had secretly hoped that Diarmid would be killed in the encounter with this boar, and thus his problems would be solved, said that the measurement could not be right, and asked Diarmid to pace it again the other way. Diarmid did as he was bid, but this time a poisonous bristle pricked his heel, and he fell dying.

Fingal, who had deeply loved the young man, was stricken sore at this agony, and asked what he could to cure him. Conveniently there was a spring with magical powers close by, and Diarmid asked that Fingal should himself bring water in his hands, saying that this would cure the poisonous wound. Twice Fingal tried, but each time when his cupped hands were filled with the magical water, he was so gripped with anger at the treachery of his beautiful Grainne that his hands shook and the water spilled to the ground. A third time he tried, and he firmly drove all thoughts of Grainne from his mind and hurried back to Diarmid. Too late, the young man was dead, and Fingal was filled with remorse at the death of one he had loved.

Just then some other men of Fingal's band came from the forest bringing Grainne with them. She had told them, and they told their chief, that during all their wanderings together, Diarmid had never lain with her, but had treated her always with the respect due to the wife of his chief. Fingal refused even to look at her, far less listen to her, and ordered that she be killed instantly. This was done, and once again, but in death now, Grainne and her beloved, but unattainable, Diarmid were reunited.

A pretty tale indeed, and it is commemorated to this day on the Campbell flag, which depicts a boar's head, for Diarmid is said to have been the progenitor of that great family. And commemorated, too, by the name of the hill, for *Beinn an Tuirc* means the Hill of the Boar.

Just south of Carradale where the road winds down to Saddell Bay, there are the ruins of another castle and an abbey. Of the two, the Abbey is much the finer. It was a Cistercian foundation, and is very old. So old that it might have been founded by Somerled himself in 1160.

Somerled was assassinated at Dumbarton, and was brought here, is it believed, to lie in one of the tombs. His son, Reginald, is said to have sent to Rome for a quantity of consecrated dust, which he sprinkled on the ground in the outline of a great cross, and ordered that the Abbey be extended to fill that outline.

Like all Cistercian foundations, the monks at Saddell were great agriculturalists, and greedy for land, and eventually their endowment extended to Arran and Bute. There is not much of the Abbey left now -- like most other abbeys it was used as a convenient source of ready-dressed building stone by everyone in the district -- but it lies fine and quiet by a burn tumbling out of the hills. That is *Allt nam Monach*, the Monks Burn, and it flows through *Bealach nam Barbh*, the Pass of the Dead, over which bodies from the west of Kintyre were carried for burial at Saddell Abbey.

Although so ruinous today that it is difficult to distinguish its original size and shape, the choir can still be seen, and it contains a large number of most beautifully carved burial slabs with galleys, hounds, stags and armed warriors. There is no knowing who rests beneath them, but those stones are very fine and evocative, and a visit there to wander for an hour amongst those relics of a past long dead is a fine thing to remember.

A little south again is Ugadale, and there is another story of King Robert Bruce connected with Ugadale. The very night after he had been kept warm by the goat on Sliab h-Gaoil, the wandering king was given shelter by a man called McKay, who did not recognise him. On being told that he must sit for his meal, the king replied that 'must' is a word that only kings should use to their subjects. 'Every man is a king in his own house,' replied McKay, and so the king sat to his supper. He did not forget, and gave MacKay a silver brooch with a large cairngorm, and later, when he was securely on the throne granted the man the land he farmed. That precious brooch is still in the possession of McKay's descendants.

By now, you are almost in Campbeltown, and Campbeltown Loch is opening up. There is another ruined church, though, at Kilchausland. That is worthy of a visit, if only for its setting. It stands on a cliff surrounded by its churchyard, and looks out to distant Ayrshire, Ailsa Craig and nearby Arran. Right below is Davaar Island, brown and threatening, guarding and sheltering the entrance to Campbeltown Loch.

The church, of which a good deal still stands in spite of its very exposed position, was dedicated to St. Causlan. There are many fine old stones in the churchyard, but the most famous one is missing. It was described in a guidebook of a hundred years ago, but has since vanished. This was the marrying stone. It was a pillar pierced by a hole just big enough for a hand to pass through, and any eloping couple who managed to reach the church and join hands through it was held to be legally and properly married. The legend is that this was approved by no less an authority than St. Causlan himself, who held that a promise of marriage was as binding as any marriage service.

That view of an indissoluble marriage was not shared by St. Causlan's near neighbour, St. Coivan, whose chapel was just a few miles away, between Campbeltown and Machrihanish. St. Coivan had a much more robust view of things -- perhaps more realistic, too.

On a particular midnight each year, all who were discontented with their marriage could repair to St. Coivan's church, where each was blindfolded and left to move around the church. Then St. Coivan called out '**Gubhag**' -- Seize -- and every man had to take hold of the nearest woman, and that woman was his wife for the next twelve months at least, and until discontent again arose. It sounds like the alleged happenings in today's suburbia.

Just south of Kilchausland, the road climbs steeply, and from the summit there is the best view of the town and the loch. From that point one can also see, if the tide is low, the curving shingle ridge that allows one to reach Davaar Island dryshod. It cannot be stressed too strongly that the mile-long walk over that shingle ridge (known as *An Dorlinn*) should not be undertaken lightly. The tide runs fast there and covers the shingle quickly once it has turned. Do check with local people before you walk out.

Davaar is uninhabited, and the sudden appearance of a cave painting there in 1887 was a mystery and remained so for some years. It was then found to be the work of a young local artist, Alexander Mackinnon, and Mackinnon himself, by then 80 years old, went again to the cave in 1934 to retouch and finish his Crucifixion scene. You can find the cave easily enough -- it is the fifth of the seven caves in the cliffs -- and will surely feel that the painting well fits the peacefulness of the cave.

Even apart from the interesting wall painting, a visit to Davaar is fascinating because of the splendid natural rock gardens there. The cliffs support such a wealth of plants that surely no man-made rockery can compete. The colours are gentle and subdued, and the plants cling close to the rocks, for this can be a wild coast in a storm, but on a summer day they present such a picture of natural beauty that it is unforgettable.

Campbeltown is a working town, a harbour, and as yet has seen no reason to pretty itself up as a tourist attraction. With its population of six and half thousand, it is by far the metropolis of Kintyre. It is still a busy fishing port, but, alas, there are now only two distilleries. Once there were thirty four. And there is now no coal mined.

But those two distilleries produce some of the finest and most interesting whisky in Scotland, and we should be thankful that they exist. Tradition insists that the Glen Scotia distillery stands on the site of a once famous illicit still, and you will find no-one to deny that the malthouse is haunted even today by the uneasy ghost of MacCallum, one of the early proprietors, who took his own life by drowning in Campbeltown loch after being swindled by some unscrupulous characters from south of the border.

The Campbeltown Cross, at the pier head, is a very fine and richly carved Celtic Cross. By immemorial custom, all funerals in the town detour past the Cross. This is perhaps the finest piece of medieval carving in the whole of Kintyre. It was created about 1380 to the memory of one Ivor MacEarchearn, and in 1609, when Campbeltown became a Royal Burgh, it was moved to act as the market cross. The central carving was probably a Crucifixion, but that cannot be traced now. There is a Madonna, and some saints, whilst on the other side there are strange monsters, including one with two bodies and only one head. There is also something that looks remarkably like a mermaid.

If your interest is in the past, then surely you will want to visit the small Campbeltown museum in the public library. It has an excellent archeological collection of finds from all over Kintyre. And no part of Britain is so rich in relics of a distant past as this one. From the Neolithic farmers of five thousand years ago, to post-Reformation graves of the 17th and 18th centuries, the eternal stones of Kintyre give us a rich tapestry of life and death down the ages. The local Tourist Information Office has published a concise but very interesting booklet "Guide For Visitors" which lists many of

the archeological sites, and this is well worth while for those whose interests lie in that direction.

It is no great distance from Campbeltown further south to the Mull of Kintyre and Southend, and the circular trip is grand. There is a direct road, B842, between Campbeltown and Southend, but much finer is the old coast road to the east. It lifts and plunges, sometimes skirting the sea, sometimes running along the edge of great cliffs, with wonderful views across the Firth of Clyde. Perhaps this is the very best part of the whole east coast road from Tarbert.

As one approachs the Mull, the nature of the country changes. There are wide moors, and delightful glens running down to the sea, with a rich tapestry of colour and the smell of seaweed and the cry of birds. Wholly delightful.

There is a grand view of Southend from the last hill on the road. It lies along a curving sandy shore, with Dunaverty Rock cradled there, and Ireland lying only a dozen miles away. It is a sleepy enough place today, but once history was made here, for on the top of Dunaverty Rock are the ruins of a great stronghold, once the seat of power of the MacDonalds, Lords of the Isles. There are records indicating that as long ago as 710 there was a fortification on Dunaverty. King Robert Bruce found sanctuary in the castle during his long months of wandering in Kintyre, and it was here that the clans set at naught the plans of King James IV to unite the whole of Scotland under his Kingship.

But it was in 1647 that Dunaverty became infamous. It was a bad time for Kintyre. The whole Peninsula had been made a desolate smoking ruin as one of the MacDonalds, Colkitto, sought to recover it for his own. The MacDonalds had never acquiesed in their loss of Kintyre, and, seizing the troubled times of the Civil War as an opportunity, they hacked their way through the land so that hardly a house or cottage was left standing. The killing was such that when it was over, there had to be a great influx of people from the Lowlands to fill the empty land.

It wasn't Colkitto who was responsible for the massacre at Dunaverty. It was General Leslie, encouraged by his chaplain, a fanatic named John Nevoy. Colkitto himself, and his equally ferocious father, had both escaped earlier from Dunaverty, the son to Ireland and the father to his castle on Islay. He was lured out of there though, and later hanged on the mast of his own galley at Dunstaffnage. Meanwhile, a garrison of three hundred MacDonalds and MacDougalls remained at Dunaverty, a constant threat to the rear of Argyll's army, even though the power of Montrose had been broken.

So Leslie besieged Dunaverty. The garrison held out until their water supply was cut off, and then surrendered to the kingdom under a flag of truce, but two days later Leslie ordered that the whole garrison be slaughtered, using the casuistry that they had surrendered to the kingdom, but not to him. And all were slaughtered, except one young man. And Dunaverty was never garrisoned or lived in again.

Carsky, beyond the grimness of Dunaverty, on the way to the lighthouse, has perhaps the finest sweep of golden sands in the whole of Kintyre although that can be argued. There is the ruin of an ancient church nearby, beneath Keill Point, and close by that ancient church is the ruin of an even older cell or chapel. It is believed that this is the original chapel of St. Columba, and nearby is a flat rock with two footprints cut into it. This is claimed to be the first place on which Columba set foot in Scotland, with what tremendous import we know. There are some who doubt that these footprints are those of St. Columba, and claim that, more probably, they mark the site of an ancient ceremony of kingship, like the remarkable footprint on the top of Dunadd Castle. What ever its origin, it is a thing, simple and undistinguished, of great antiquity, and very moving in its mystery and simplicity.

This road out to the lighthouse is really very strange. It runs at first by the shore, through great riches of vegetation, almost tropical in their luxuriance, and with wonderful seascapes, over the channel to Sanda, Rathlin and Ireland. It twists and turns, then abruptly sheers upwards on the steep slopes of Beinn na Lice, up to almost 1000 feet, where only the very toughest heather can find a roothold in the rocks. It is a bare landscape, lashed by great storms and winds, and in almost frightening contrast to the lushness below. At 1350 feet there is a narrow pass, called The Gap, and this is the end of the road, unless you are going to visit the lighthouse itself.

If you are going down there, it is a very steep corkscrew track to where the lighthouse stands, 300 feet above the sea on a vast cliff, but looking, from The Gap, like some child's toy.

This is not the first light on these great cliffs. The first was built in 1788, but the Stevensons, those remarkable builders, erected the present one in 1820. The view from the lantern on a bright day is superb, but a sunset viewed from the lantern is splendid beyond words. Perhaps it is that, apart from the tower on which you stand, there is nothing man-made to be seen. Everything is pristine and delightful and new-minted, with the colours bright like jewels, and only the mournfulness of the sea birds and the unending sough of the waves of the rocks far below to break a stillness like that of the seventh day of creation.

But stand on that lantern on a day of winter storm. Feel the whole great tower vibrate as the wind lashes it and feel it tremble as the very earth trembles when the mountainous Atlantic waves break in thunder far below. Then you can truly appreciate the forces of nature.

Returning, you do not have to go back to Southend. In fact, unusually for Kintyre, you have a choice of roads. Going back towards Southend, take the first left and first left again to go through Breakorie, or first left then second left for Connie Glen. It is hard to choose, really, although my personal fancy is for Glen Breakorie: it is more hilly, and perhaps the views are better. Actually the two routes join again just a few miles south of Campbeltown. The road to Machrihanish branches off to the left.

Machrihanish is at the southern end of the astonishing sweep of Machrihanish Bay, the longest stretch of sand and dunes in mainland Argyll. It is lovely, and sometimes frightening. There is only the 'steepe Atlantik Stream' between Machrihanish and Newfoundland, and great waves come marching in there, rolling and swaggering on the stillest of days. The dunes are vast, with machair grass struggling to live on them. It is a truly wonderful place to spend a hot summer day, with the dunes trapping the sun, the waves thundering on the beach, larks singing, and six miles of sand to wander along, beachcombing and idling through the pools.

If you have diverted off the main road to visit Machrihanish -- and it is strongly recommended that you do -- you do not have to return to Campbeltown, but instead can take the first road on the left out of Machrihanish, which will lead you up to join the main road north (A83) near Kilkenzie. A little further on is Westport, at the north end of the remarkable Machrihanish Bay, and indeed you might find that end of the Bay more to your taste, since it tends to have even fewer people around.

North, then, but on a main road now, up the more gentle west side of Kintyre. The map will show that you pass through the village of Bellochantuy. This name is another perversion forced on us by

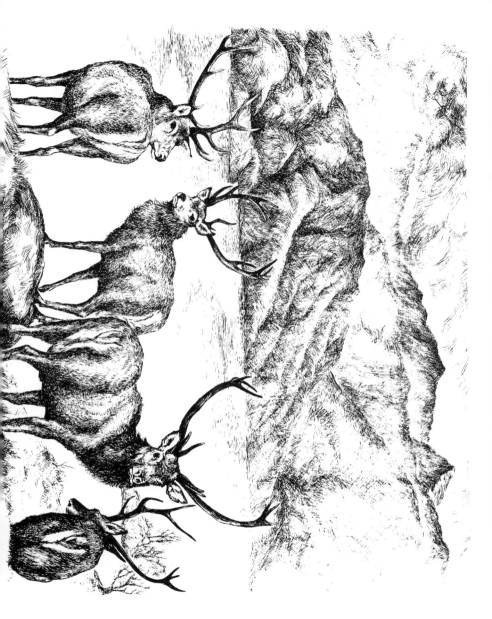

RED DEER

ignorant makers of maps. It should properly be *Bealach an t-sith*, which means 'The Fairies' Pass'. Far too many lovely Gaelic names are disappearing in this way, scuppered by cartographers complacent in their incomprehension. If they must use English for Gaelic names (and I do not see why they should), then let them translate the name, not corrupt it to some meaningless jumble of sound. William Neill, a poet of today from South-west Scotland, has written in protest about this:-

> The cold men in the city
> who circumscribe all latitude
> wiped their bullseye glasses
> laid down their stabbing pens
> that had dealt the mortal wounds
> slaying the history of a thousand years
> in the hour between lunch and catching the evening
> train.

As a matter of fact, the view from the Fairies' Pass is as fine as anything in Elfland, and the name is certainly fitting.

There is another fine beach here, running two miles or so north along the coast, and it is wonderful to stroll there in the gloaming, watching the softness of Islay dim over the western sea.

The road here runs on a raised beach, showing how the level of the sea has changed since these hills and glens were gouged by the last great Ice Age. The whole west coast is much more productive and fertile than the east coast, with all its lonely grandeur. From the dawn of history man has found a home on this kindly land, and still does.

There are four ancient sites very close to the village of the Fairies' Pass. And those are the ones we can see today: who can know how many have been destroyed and lost over the many centuries since our ancient ancestors gathered stones and slabs and erected their strong points on these hill tops?

Quite clearly, from the sites we can visit today, Kintyre in the dawn of history was well populated, and that population was well organised into a society of which we can know nothing.

It is not that these sites are all forts. The Ballocroy standing stones are aligned with the summer solstice, and clearly were an important lunar and solar observatory. We do not even know why those mysterious people needed to measure the passage of the years by the position of the sun. It is not enough to say that this dictated their sowing and mowing. No farmer, then or now, could work by the calendar or the position of the sun in its journeys. Farmers work, then and now, by the condition of the soil, its warmth, its moisture and whether they feel like taking the tractor or the digging stick to the fields that particular day.

Today, this whole west coast of Kintyre is rich agricultural land, growing mixed crops and supporting fine herds of cattle. In the days of old, it must have been a very tempting target for roving

Norse raiders, and one can well understand why the population needed so many strong points and forts.

At Glenbarr village a very minor road runs off to the right, up Barr Glen and into Carradale Forest. It is a grand road, with the rich glen on one side and bare hills and moors on the others. It is not a through road: there is no through road across the rocky spine of Kintyre.

There is a new Macalister Clan Centre at Glenbarr, in the Abbey there. The building itself is interesting, being basically a straightforward Laird's House of the late 18th Century, with the addition of a Gothic Revival wing in 1815. It sounds like a recipe for architectural disaster, but in fact it has worked quite well, producing a building of some harmony in a grand site.

All are welcome to visit, of course, Macalisters or not, and can enjoy the grounds as well as the house. And naturally, if you are a Macalister, or one of the many septs of that clan, you can be sure of a particularly warm welcome, and a pressing invitation to join the Clan Society. But you don't have to be a Macalister to enjoy the Clan Centre -- the old animosities are dead.

The ferry for Gigha leaves from Tayinloan, and if time permits, a trip over there can fill a fascinating and satisfying day.

The ancient chapel of Killean stands just to the left of the road, immediately before the ferry road for Gigha. This is of late Norman construction, and very well preserved. The Decorated windows, in the east gable, are of later design, but blend well with the sombre Norman architecture. There is a vault in the chapel, the Largie vault, and here, protected at last from the wind and the weather, is a collection of superb carved stones, superb even by the standards of the west of Scotland. They are are very much worth seeing.

Largie itself is near Tayinloan, and it has been held by the same MacDonald family from the days of Somerled himself.

This road, the A83, has been much improved of recent years, if

that is the right word, and it by-passes most of the villages. That is fine if you are in a hurry, but the holiday-maker in Kintyre should never be in a hurry, and will find it very worth while to ignore the bypasses and explore the villages.

Clachan is one such by-passed village, and is much the better for it. Now you can can visit there in comfort and look at the old church and churchyard.

So many seals congregate on a rock reef close inshore near Clachan that a special lay-by has been built where you can pull off the road and watch perhaps hundreds of Atlantic seals lolling at ease on the rocks. These waters are still rich with fish, and very attractive for seals, who gather on those tide-washed rocks to rest and sleep. Seals are no strangers to anyone who looks at the coast round Kintyre, but it is unusual to see them in such large numbers, and so unafraid.

From Clachan, or the bypass, the main road climbs steeply again over the spine of Kintyre. The West Loch is there in sight again, but not that alone. The view is very open, way to the north, to mid-Argyll, to the islands on both sides of Kintyre, and far south over that vast rugged wasteland that makes up the Kintyre peninsula.

By now, you are on the last few miles of this circumnavigation of Kintyre, heading back for Tarbert and the road north. But it is sure that you will not leave it without regret, for this is one of the most lovely of all places in Scotland. It is certain that you will carry with you memories of rare delights, and of beauty sometimes indescribable. Kintyre has had a storm-tossed history, a history of blood and battle, of treachery and compassion. But, then, that is the story of the Highlands. Out of that history has sprung a people of great resourcefulness, living in a land of splendour. Those who visit that land can only be in awe of it, and sometimes silent in the face of its beauty.

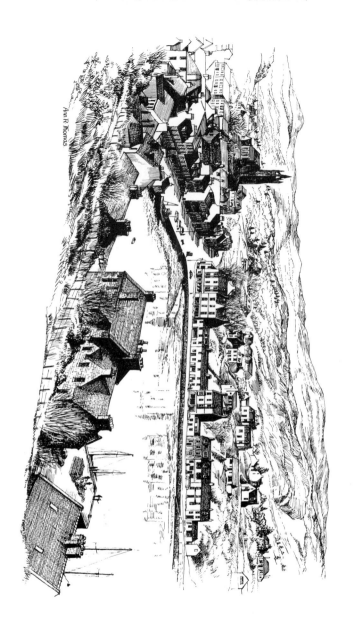

TARBERT FROM THE CASTLE

GIGHA, JURA & ISLAY

This book is not really about the islands, but it seems proper to mention them, since they can be visited in a day from Kintyre. However, you can see only a fraction of even tiny Gigha in a day's visit.

The ferry for Gigha leaves from Tayinloan. *Gigha* is a Norse name, and, roughly, means 'God's Island'. Although so tiny, it has had a stormy history, and indeed was an integral part of the Norse empire until the 14th cent. Since it is only six miles long and one mile across, it is not worth taking your car over: everything can be better reached on foot.

Gigha is a fertile and prosperous little island, with small farms, mostly dairy, using its fertile soil. Cheese is one of the main products, and a fine strong product it is. Achamore House Gardens, at the southern end of the island's only road, would of itself make a visit worthwhile at any time of year, but best of all, perhaps, in the spring. Rhododendrons and azaleas flourish there in wild abundance, as they always do in the mild west coast climate, but there is much more than that at Achamore. Magnolias, camellias and viburnums are there, and the walled garden is a glory of roses and much else. There are fifty acres of garden, and the walk through them is two miles long. And it is never crowded. A very fine expedition.

The ruins of the 13th cent. Cilchattan church are also well worth visiting, but surely the best of Gigha is to be found simply by wandering more or less idly and absorbing the quietness.

Islay is a much bigger and more populated island, with car ferries going from Kenacraig on West Loch Tarbert to both Port Ellen (south of the island) and Port Askaig (north). It is difficult to

LAPHROAIG

FAR AND AWAY THE MOST DISTINCTIVE MALT WHISKY.

Laphroaig is a distinguished malt whisky which inherits its distinctive rich and smoky taste from the traditional Isle of Islay distillery.

SINGLE ISLAY MALT AS UNIQUE AS THE ISLAND ITSELF.

say which is preferable, but if you plan to cross to Jura, then you must take the ferry to Port Askaig, where a passenger ferry connects for Jura.

Certainly that trip to Port Askaig is very fine, especially as the route runs right through the lovely Sound of Islay, with Islay on one side and the great hills of Jura on the other.

It is quite a long and certainly expensive trip to Islay, but overwhelmingly worth while, for it is as yet an 'undiscovered' island, and quiet, as Skye, now so busy, was once quiet.

To many, 'Islay' and 'whisky' are almost synonomous. This is dangerous ground to tread, perhaps, but there are many, including myself, who are convinced that Scotland's best whisky comes from Islay. This is not the properly scorned blends sold over every bar, which are mixtures of real malt whisky with an unknown amount of tasteless spirit manufactured from maize, chiefly. No, the whisky of Islay is made only from malt, exposed gently to the smoke of Islay peat, and then reverently distilled in copper stills of age and beauty. The result is a drink satisfying to all the senses, from the sounding of the cork coming gladly from the bottle to the fine peat-laden aroma, the gentle fire of the taste and the touch of the delicate oiliness on the tongue. Quite delectable, although, like most delights, the price is not negligible.

Islay, the Queen of the Isles, is rich land, low-lying (mostly), and fruitful, and crops ripen early here in the long summer days. Old Ptolemy wrote of Islay, and noted that it was famous for horses. He was right, although you will see few horses these days. There is an old Gaelic saying that an Islay man would carry a saddle and bridle a mile and a half, to ride half a mile!

The Lords of the Isles were centred on Islay. They were proclaimed -- for they were in fact kings -- on an island in Loch Finlaggan, just south of Port Askaig on A846. That island (the larger one in the Loch) is rich in ancient burial slabs, very beautifully carved. The belief is that these were the graves of women and children of chiefs, while the chiefs themselves were taken to Iona for burial. There are the ruins of an old chapel and some other buildings on the island.

A few yards away is another, smaller, island, and this was the place of council, where the Lord of the Isles sat on a square stone, with his chiefs and priests, his Council of Sixteen, around him.

A continuing archeological dig here is uncovering new evidence of a very considerable centre of an unexpected civilisation. After all, this was the seat of an important kingdom, or lordship, and medieval buildings of dressed stone and lime mortar are being uncovered. There was a Great Hall, comparable in size to that of Linlithgow Palace, and remains of much industrial activity. It was probably in that Great Hall that the Lords of the Isles made their fateful decision, at the end of the 15th. Century, to assist the English, to invade the Scottish mainland, and divide the country between them. It was an ill-fated decision, and the result was that Iain, the Lord of the Isles, and his son Iain, were both hanged in Edinburgh.

Way to the south end of Islay, just west of Port Ellen, there are the dark ruins of Dun Naomhaig, which the cartographers, in their ignorance, have re-named Dunyveg. This was a stronghold of the MacDonalds, Lords of the Isles, and when their glory had departed, it saw some troubled times. Once, it was captured by the enemies of old Coll Ciotach -- Left Handed Coll -- while he was away. Coll's piper was amongst the prisoners, but he managed to play a warning tune on his pipes as the unsuspecting Coll approached, and Coll escaped, to die another day. But the piper had played his last tune, for his right hand was cut off, and never again could he play the pipes. The tune he played to warn his chief was *Colla no Run,* and it is a tune played to this day.

The ancient ruin of Kildalton chapel, with the lovely Kildalton Cross, are on this same road. Around the Cross there are many burial slabs of great age, some of them showing old warriors with their great two-handled swords. It was at Kildalton that St. Columba is believed to have landed when he left Ireland, although, in truth, he seems to have landed at many places. There is also a Sanctuary Cross at Kildalton. Any fugitive who reached a sanctuary was safe from his enemies, for he was protected by the power of the saints. Moreover, if he stayed for a year and a day by the Cross, then he was safe to go wherever he wished, and would be unhindered.

Much of Islay is fine rolling land, except for the roadless mass of the south-east. But south-west of Port Ellen is the bare savagery of the Mull of Oa. That is a wild and rock-bound shore, facing all the great Atlantic storms. This was where the liner *'Tuscania'* struck with great loss of life. That was during the First World War, and the ship was carrying American troops to France. It was a dark night of storm, and she struck some of those great black rock fangs that jut so menacingly from even a calm sea. Many hundreds of lives, British and American, were lost on the cliffs of the Mull of Oa that night. The American Red Cross erected a monument there, a tower, which faces the cliffs and the jagged rocks where so many died during those fearful hours of darkness and storm.

Jura is an island that seems to dominate everything in the Inner Hebrides, chiefly perhaps because of its mountains. These are the lovely, shapely, Paps of Jura, so famed in Gaelic song and story. A car ferry runs to the island from Port Askaig, and the single minor road on the island runs up the east coast almost to the northern tip. The Norsemen named the island *Dyrey,* and a thousand years ago they knew it well, and hunted the red deer, bringing their feared galleys deep into sheltered Loch Tarbert, which almost cuts the island in two.

A traveller of the 17th cent., Sir James Turner, did not have a good word to say for the Island. 'Jura', he wrote, 'a horid ile and a habitation for deere and wild beasts.' Of course, that was in the days when all the Highlands and Islands were hardly better known than the depths of the Brazilian jungle are today, and when it was quite seriously held in England that Highlandmen had tails! Today, Jura is still an island fit for deer and wild beasts, and they are still there. But it is also an oasis of tranquillity in a restless world.

It is an island with a sad history. Once well populated with a people living a life balanced with nature, today it is empty, and the glens once lively with black cattle and children are deserted and echo only to the roaring of stags. At the beginning of the 19th cent. 1000 cattle were exported every year from Jura and almost 1000 people lived there. Then came the 'White Plague' of the sheep, as landowners with only a tenuous legal right drove out the people and their cattle and settled sheep in their place, sheep which destroyed the fertility of the land, and left desolation behind them when, in their turn, they were moved to make way for 'sporting estates', owned by those who had no sense of history, and no loyalty to the remaining people. In its small way, Jura was a microcosm of what happened in the Highlands and Islands when clan loyalties were destroyed and a whole society was destroyed, by those, many of them hereditary clan chiefs, intent only on seeking the maximum cash return.

Today, only a fifth as many people live on Jura as in the 18th cent., and they do not find it easy. Man cannot live on beauty and history: bread, too, is needed.

One of the strange things about Jura is the reputation it has for the longevity of the people living there. There are many tales about this, and also some evidence of it, for in the old burial ground at Inverlassa, at the north of the island, is a stone with this inscription:-

Mary MacCrain, died 1856, aged 128. Descendent of Gillour MacCrain, who kept 180 Christmases in his own house, and who died in the reign of Charles I.'

If you can, and time permits, do climb one or other of Jura's mountains. The views are superb, from the Isle of Man to the Outer Hebrides, and over all the mountains and glens of the mainland, and over to Arran. But it is not only distant views of the high hills that entrance the eye. Under your feet, heather and milkwort will be in flower. There is bright moss and the icy white stars of saxifrage. A whole delightful, sensuous, world of colour and smell is on those hillsides, bleak though they may seem from below.

There are many caves along the uninhabited north and west

coasts of the island, and a happy day can be spent beachcombing along those shores and (with care) exploring those caves.

At the north of the island, between Jura and Scarba, is the ferocious whirlpool of Corrievreckan, or, properly *Coire Bhreacain.* There are strong tides racing through this narrow channel every day, and tremendous tide-rips. A place to be avoided in any boat and the graveyard of many over the years. So loud is the roar of the waters meeting and struggling there that it can sometimes be heard on the mainland.

The Second Statistical Account of Scotland recounts an old legend of how the whirlpool got its name. It derived, the legend holds, from one Prince Breachkan, from Norway, who, on one of his visits to the islands, met and fell in love with a young Princess of the Isles, and sought to marry her. Her father did not wish this, but, fearful of crossing the desires of such a powerful Prince, finally gave his consent, provided that the young man prove himself by anchoring his galley for three days in the whirlpool.

The young Prince returned home and prepared for his trial. He had three great cables made, one of hemp, one of wool and one of the hair from women, for his sages assured him that nothing would break this last, for the purity of women's innocence would overcome the power of the waves. The women of his country so loved Breachkan that they gladly gave up their hair for him.

He returned to Jura, and sailed to the whirlpool at slack tide when the water is calm. He put down a great anchor on the hemp rope, but on the first day the cable parted. He put down the woollen rope, but on the second day it snapped. He put down the rope of hair with his last anchor, but was not worried, for he trusted the wisdom of his sages and the innocence of his women. The third rope snapped, weakened by the hair of one who was *not* innocent, and in the fearful maelstrom Breachkan's galley was driven ashore and smashed and the young Prince drowned. His body was dragged ashore by his faithful dog, and buried in a cave nearby.

A grand legend, but more probably, if mundanely, the name

comes from the Gaelic for Speckled (or Brindled) Corrie, and that is a good and descriptive name, as you can see when the tide begins to set, and the smooth hurrying water is speckled with tiny whirls before they coalesce into the great hungry mouth of the Cailleach (Old Woman), as the local people used to call Corrievreckan.

Lest you think that local tales and warnings about the peculiar ferocity of Corrievreckan are exaggerated, be assured that they are not. More than one modern and powerful boat has vanished in those seas, leaving only bits of scattered wreckage to be recovered. The final, and most powerful warning, which I have noted before, but cannot stress too often, is contained in the Admiralty publication *The West Coast of Scotland Pilot*. **'Navigation is at times most hazardous and no stranger under any circumstances can be justified in attempting it.'**

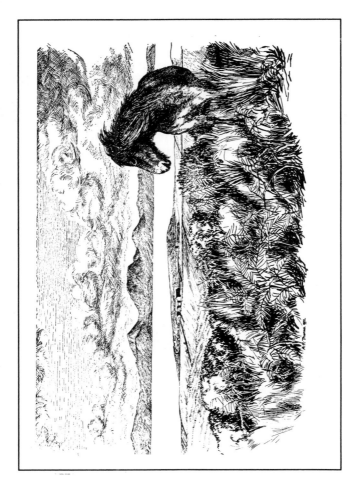

PAPS OF JURA

LOCH FYNE, LOCH ECK, INVERARAY & CENTRAL ARGYLL

From Lochgilphead the A83 runs up the west side of Loch Fyne to Inveraray and round the head of the Loch. Lochgilphead itself is a pleasant town, with a most excellent outlook over Loch Gilp when the tide is in. And of course it is an excellent centre for those exploring Knapdale and touring Kintyre. It is a town planned

and built from nothing -- a 'greenfield site'-- by the local proprietor at the beginning of the 19th cent. The high hopes for attracting people and industry did not materialise, and there is little of the fishing left. Today it is a market town, and retains all the openness and airiness that the original designer built into it.

The Parish Church, at the top of the main street, has a very fine set of stained glass windows. There are three of them, telling the story of the Nativity, and they glow delightful and fresh. They were designed by Sir Edward Burne-Jones, who was one of the pillars of the pre-Raphaelite Movement which did so much to improve design in late-Victorian Britain.

To go north on the A83 you must first go south for a few miles, down Loch Gilp to Loch Fyne. The road doesn't follow the coast very closely, and if it happens that you are seeking great sweeps of empty beaches, and fine sandy ones at that, then leave the main road and go down to the coast at Castleton, and walk from there in either direction along some of the best beaches in all of Argyll.

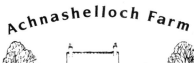

Once Castleton and Port Ann and Loch Gair, a little further north, were all busy and prosperous fishing villages, but that has all gone today.

The road up Loch Fyne is very pretty, running through the fertile plains beside the loch, and looking over the mile of salt water to Glendaruel and the hills of Cowal. Across the loch, the old grey walls of Castle Lachlan still brood as they have done for so long.

At Crarae there are some of the finest gardens in Scotland. These are on the Cumlodden Estate, about 12 miles south of Inveraray, and just a little further from Lochgilphead. They are not old gardens, dating only from the early years of this century, and consequently do not have the great wealth of mature trees that older gardens have, but there is a most spectacular display of very unusual plants and shrubs. Because it is in the Western Highlands, where these things flourish so wonderfully well, the show of rhododendrons and azaleas is particularly impressive. There are some very fine walks laid out in the gardens, and altogether one can spend some happy hours there. Three generations of the Campbell family have devoted their lives to building this woodland paradise, and the love and skill have well paid off. In the gardens, incidentally, there is a very fine chambered burial cairn, in which the remains of both cremations and burials were found.

A little further north again is Furnace, where there are the ruins of an 18th cent. iron smelting plant and a great granite quarry. This iron furnace was one of these established to exploit the great forests of the Highlands, and thus were responsible for much of the denudation of these now gaunt hills. When the forests were felled, the furnaces cooled and the industry moved away.

There was a gunpowder mill here, too, also using the local charcoal, but there was a dreadful explosion in the mill in 1883, and that was the end of that.

The main road leaves the loch at Furnace -- although there is a track round the headland -- and goes inland to Auchindrain. This was a very important junction for the old cattle drovers in days past, and today you can follow their still well-defined tracks west to the distant coast or north to Loch Awe. They are foot-tracks, of course.

The last joint-tenancy, run-rig farm in Scotland was at Auchindrain, and it ceased being a working farm only in 1963. Today, it has been restored as a museum, and very fine it is. The joint tenancy farms were hardly farms as we think of them today: they were communities of families, each of which paid a proportion of the rent, determined by the amount and quality of the land they worked. Each family held a number of unfenced strips in both the infield and outfield land, and these were re-allocated each year. The rents of those farms were often paid in kind, rather than in cash, and the tenants had no security of tenure. Also, they were subject to many restrictions on what they must or must not do.

It was from these joint-tenancy farms that the women and young people, with the animals, moved out each summer to the shielings on the high hills, while the men concentrated on sowing and gathering the crops.

It is the slim folk-memory of those summer shielings that is responsible for much of the misty romanticism dreamed of the Highlands. In reality, for the women and youngsters, and for the men, the whole way of life was unbelievably hard and brutal, and there was little romance about it.

Certainly there was much to be said for the social values of those communities, which cared for the old and destitute and shared their poverty equally. And there was much to be said for the rich Gaelic culture of song and poetry and story that they cherished. But it was a harsh and short life, and it is well that it has gone into the romantic mists of legend.

But to return to Auchindrain. This museum is fine, with several cruck and truss buildings dating from about 1770, and by a little stretch of the imagination one can see what life was like for the ordinary people of the Highlands. The ordinary people, not those who lived in castles or counted their wealth by the tens of thousands of acres and houses in London. Of course, the filth and the smell, the smoke and the hunger, cannot be seen, but we know of those anyway.

The road then rejoins the coast, and runs north again to Inveraray. The last wolf in Argyll was killed by a woman near Auchindrain, just where the old bridge crosses the Leachan Water. Unfortunately, the woman died, too, from shock, but had killed the wolf by stabbing it with her spindle.

Inveraray is a strange little town to find in the Highlands. Virtually, it is a Georgian town, set on the shores of Loch Fyne, in a situation of grandeur, dominated by a massive, quite new castle, basically classical in design, but iced with Gothic decoration.

Inveraray is the seat of the Campbells, headed by the Duke of Argyll, and one cannot ever forget that. MacCailein Mor, the Campbell chief, moved his headquarters to Inveraray from Loch Awe in the 15th cent., and he built the first castle there. That is not what one sees today. The present castle, and indeed the town, dates from 1745, when the Duke, tired of the old, cold building in which he lived, decided to build a new residence, modern, and in keeping with his status. He considered that the old town was too close to the site he chose for his castle, so he demolished the town and had it rebuilt, new and gleaming, where it now stands. That was the sort of thing a Duke of Argyll could decide before breakfast.

The present castle was designed by Roger Morris, who had learned his trade by working with Vanburgh, and the building was supervised by William Adam and his famous sons. There was a serious fire at the castle in 1975, and much damage was done, but some of the State rooms have been restored now, and are again open.

Perhaps the most striking sight in the castle is the great armoury in the central hall, with all the weapons displayed in decorative patterns, a peculiar sort of conceit one finds in many Scottish castles. Many of these weapons, though, were the very ones supplied to the Campbell troops in 1715 and again in 1745, when they went to fight against the gallant, romantic and utterly daft Jacobite rebellions.

INVERARAY

Ann R Thomas

The gardens of the castle are fine, with truly magnificent trees, some of them the finest and biggest of their kind in Britain. A rather stiff walk will take you to the top of Dun Cuaich, once the site of an ancient fort, but now topped by a delightful watch tower, designed by Morris. Since this was built after the defeat of the 1745 rebellion, it was more in the nature of a summer house than a real watch tower -- there was no one left to watch for -- and the views from it are magnificent in every direction. Sir Walter Scott climbed to the top of the hill and described it as:-

'.....a picturesque peak starting abruptly from the lake, and raising its scathed brow into the mists of middle sky, while a solitary watch tower perched on its top like an eagle's nest gave dignity to the scene by awakening a sense of possible danger.'

But Sir Walter was ever an ultra-romantic.

A new museum in the castle grounds commemorates the days in the last war when Inveraray served as a training centre for Commando and Combined Operation troops, many thousands of whom prepared for battle on these hills and that loch.

The ubiquitous Johnson and Boswell stayed in Inveraray, and Boswell records that there Johnson for the first time drank whisky, saying that he wanted to know what it was that makes a Scotchman (sic) happy. They stayed at the inn and found it comfortable, but dined at the castle, where Boswell was repeatedly snubbed by his noble hostess.

Another visitor to the hotel at Inveraray was Robert Burns, but he was not impressed. He used his ever-present diamond to write on one of the windows:-

> There's naething here but Hielan' pride,
> An' Hieland scab and hunger:
> If Providence has sent me here,
> 'Twere surely in his anger.

It is said that the owners of the inn were so busy with the incipient arrival of some member of the Argyll family that they could not attend to the more simple requirements of the Poet.

See the town in the very early morning, if you can, or perhaps in the late evening, after the coaches have gone their noisy way. It is a charming place, white and gleaming, and well proportioned.

But until recently it cannot have had much charm for the inhabitants, even though it is close under the castle walls. In 1958 a survey showed that of 103 houses, only 13 had bathrooms, and 22 had indoor toilets. Different now, of course.

The court room is still there, the one where James of the Glen was tried in 1752 for the murder of Campbell of Glenure, tried and convicted by a Campbell judge and a Campbell jury and hanged in his own country of Ballachulish for a murder he did not commit.

The little double church is also still there, double because half was used for Gaelic services and half for English. The Episcopal Church within the castle grounds, has a very fine bell tower, built in red granite to a Gothic design as a memorial to the many Campbells killed in the First World War. A grand thought, but a design that hardly fits into the general harmony of the town plan. Its peal of ten bells is very fine, one of the best in the whole of Britain.

The Inveraray Cross, on the sea front, is a superb piece of 15th cent. work, believed to have been brought from Iona. The Latin inscription states that it commemorates Duncan MacGille Com ghan, his son Patrick and Patrick's son, MacGill Maire.

A graceful bridge over the river, now preserved and by-passed, complements a group of buildings that are, mostly, very pleasing to the eye, even if the idea of Palladian construction in the Highlands does seem somewhat fanciful.

Neil Munro was born in Crombie's Land at Inveraray, and surely no writer has done more to recreate, through his artistry, days long gone. *John Splendid, Doom Castle* and *The New Road* are fine novels. He wrote, too, very vividly, about his own youth in Inveraray, and about the characters in the town. One was the retired skipper who was the general factotum, being harbour master, lamplighter, bell-ringer, streetsweeper and grave- digger!

Strangely, Neil Munro is best remembered not for his novels

or memoirs, but for the immortal Para Handy and other members of the crew of the *Vital Spark*. He wrote those occasional pieces for the newspaper he worked for, and thought so little of them that he did not even sign them with his own name. But they are excellent. They record incidents from the career of the *Vital Spark* and her crew. She was a steam-puffer, imaginary, of course, although everyone who lived in the Highlands and Islands of fifty years ago knew those puffers and their crew well, and will tell you that Para Handy and the rest are completely true to life. She was out of Glasgow, trading to every port and beach throughout the Islands and Highlands. Steam-puffers have gone now, and the western seaboard much poorer for it. They were great iron shoe boxes with a cabin and an engine at the back, and they could be beached anywhere, off-loaded with the derrick, and floated away again on the next tide. It was a great sight to see one of them heading in from the open sea, pushing half the loch in front of her, and with a great black plume eddying away into the distance. The tales of Para Handy, skipper of the *Vital Spark*, are quite delicious, and surely immortal.

But Neil Munro was a poet, too, and he lamented in his poetry the desolation of the Highlands after the Clearances:-

> *The friends are all departed*
> *The hearth stones black and cold,*
> *And sturdy grows the nettle*
> *On the place beloved of old.......*
> *There's deer upon the mountain,*
> *There's sheep along the glen.*
> *The forests hum with feathers*
> *But where are now the men?.....*

A good question, and the answer is that those, with their families, who had not been drowned in ships unfit to put to sea, were trying desperately to wring a living out of howling wildernesses in Canada and America and Australia.

There is a tall cairn on top of a hillock on the grand road leading from Inveraray to Loch Awe through Glen Aray. This is a

Dunderave Castle

monument to Neil Munro.

Near the headwaters of Loch Fyne there is the castle of Dunderave, or *Dun da Ramh*, the Fort of the Two Oars. This is the old seat of the MacNaughtons, one of the most ancient of Highland families. This was Munro's Castle Doom.

Between Inveraray and Dunderave a very minor road leads off to the left up the very pleasant Glen Shira. The Boshang Gate is here, and it is said that this gate got its name in an amusing way. A Frenchman, we know not whom, was the guest of the Duke at Inveraray Castle. He longed for the lushness of his native land, and found the mists and wild rivers and dark lochs of Argyll strange and frightening. One day he rode out from Inveraray to Glen Shira, which is rich and green even today, and exclaimed: *'Quel beau champs!* Ever since the gate has been known as Boshang!

Glen Shira is fertile and wooded, leading away north-east into the high hills and to the hill lochs. About five miles up the glen, nestling into the shoulder of Beinn Bhuidhe, is the ruin of Rob Roy MacGregor's house. He

lived there, an outlaw, for ten years before 1715. The roof is gone now, but the walls stand. A few years ago, Rob Roy's dirk, engraved with his initials, was found on a ledge of rock above the river Shira, and his sporran is in Inveraray Castle. It is somehow hard to realise that Rob Roy MacGregor was a real person and not just a character in a novel, and a real person whose life was even more full of tragedy and courage than the novelist has told.

Back to the main road still the A83 and it continues right round the head of Loch Fyne to Carndow. There is a choice of roads there, just through the village, with the A83 continuing up Glen Kinglas and eventually over to Tarbet on Loch Lomond. The other road goes off to the right, and as A815 runs down the east side of Loch Fyne and eventually down to Dunoon in the Cowal Peninsula. For the moment, we will continue on the A83.

This is the once notorious Rest-and-be-Thankful road, now thoroughly tamed and, if not exactly a speed track, certainly nothing to be concerned about. The old road, though, much of which is visible from the new, was something else again, and the stone marking the summit, the Rest & Be Thankful Stone, was a welcome sight to many a motorist whose radiator was blowing steam. And even more for the horses of an earlier age.

Of course, the new road still runs through the same magnificent gorge, with the great outline of The Cobbler above, and then down steeply through the Highland splendour of Glen Croe to the shores of Loch Long and over the narrow neck of land to Loch Lomond. That narrow neck of land is where the Norsemen once hauled their galleys, to relaunch them in Loch Lomond and plunder the richness there, where the people were unprepared for such an invasion.

The Cobbler gets its fanciful name because from one view the great hill resembles a cobbler bending over his last. But you do need imagination to see that.

That old road of Rest-and-be-Thankful was a military road originally, started after the 1715 rebellion, and finished after the

1745. Its purpose was to allow English troops to move quickly through the Highlands and repress any troubles. Those roads crisscross the Highlands, although there aren't many of them in Argyll, where the Duke himself could be trusted to keep the King's Peace.

For the walker, the summit of Rest-and-be-Thankful is an ideal place. There are peaks in every direction, and none of them difficult, although it must ever be remembered that these are mountains, and must be treated with great respect. The easiest way up The Cobbler is not from Rest-and-be-Thankful, although there is an obvious track from there. There is a path from Arrochar at the head of Loch Long, and that is the way advised for those perhaps not so sure of mountain walking and mountain conditions.

For now, let us leave A83 at the summit of Rest-and-be-Thankful and take the B828 on the right. This leads down, through scenes of magnificence, to Loch Goil, Lochgoilhead, and finally to Carrick Castle. For Lochgoilhead and the south, you keep left at the solitary road junction on to B839. The road twists, climbs and plunges in a very satisfactory way, and everyone, except perhaps the driver, will be enthralled by it.

The village of Lochgoilhead is in a fine sheltered spot, facing down the loch to Argyll's Bowling Green, as the great turbulent tongue of land is called, separating Loch Goil and Loch Long. For those hale and hearty enough to face it -- and it is not to be taken lightly -- one of the finest foot trails in the whole of Scotland leads right round that tongue of land. It is a walk of true splendour and loneliness, and takes you into glens and over passes where very few ever tread.

The name of Argyll's Bowling Green given on the maps for this area is strange. It is yet another corruption of the Gaelic, and properly is *Baile na Greine* -- Sunny Cattle Fold -- and applied originally to the grazing land at the south-east. Corrupted by the cartographers, it somehow strikes the right note of jest about this wild place.

There is a very puzzling sun-dial at Lochgoilhead. It is in a private garden, but a right-of-way goes to it. It stands on a pillar ten feet high, dated 1626. The red sandstone pillar is curiously carved with cup marks, hearts and other devices, and is fine. But no-one can explain how one is meant to read the dial when it is ten feet in the air!

The European Sheep and Wool Centre is at Lochgoilhead. This is housed in a custom-built theatre, and in the forty minute show you will see 19 different breeds of sheep live on stage, as well as sheep shearing and sheep dog demonstrations. We are all familiar with the popular 'One Man and his Dog' television show: here is a chance to see something rather similar live. There is also, of course, a shop with a very large selection of Scottish woollen goods.

Continuing down Loch Goil, the end of the road is reached at Carrick Castle. This is a 15th cent. castle, very impressive in both size and position. It was captured by the Marquis of Atholl in 1685, when the Earl of Argyll was in revolt, and was trounced by the Marquis. It was left roofless then, and still is. But the ruins are impressive,certainly, with two more floors above the great central hall. An unusual, and very puzzling, feature is a small chimney actually built into a window recess, for what purpose no one can now guess.

As with so many entrancing journeys in this part of Scotland, one must return the same way, up the length of Loch Goil to the road junction where B839 dives off to the left, through Hell's Glen --a place that in no way lives up to its ferocious name. It is a pleasant glen of grass and heather, and runs quite unsensationally down to the eastern shore of Loch Fyne, although the views of near hills and distant waters are grand indeed.

Not far from the road junction by the loch side, to the right, is Ardkinglas House. This is a different house, but it was to the Laird of Ardkinglas that MacIan of Glencoe came in the winter of 1692 to make his submission and swear allegiance to the King. Sir Colin Campbell administered the oath, but was then over-ruled by the King and by those in Edinburgh who had determined to make an example of some of the Highland clans, and regretted only that it was not some great and noble clan, instead of that sad and ragged remnant in Glencoe. So they slaughtered MacIan and his people, and left a stain on Scottish history that never fades.

The road down the east side of Loch Fyne (A815) is a good fast road, heading south to Dunoon and the Cowal Peninsula. But before you make off at high speed, stop a moment just where the minor road joins the main road. There is a fenced-off section of an older road there, towards the loch, and on that old road surface, still plain (indeed, preserved) a large heart is outlined with white stones. This was the place where tinkers gathered and celebrated weddings. It was a site used for many generations and no doubt still would be if there were any tinkers left.

Down Loch Fyne, with Inveraray on the opposite shore, and on, then, to Strachur. There is a very fine 18th cent. mansion here, long (but no longer) in Campbell ownership. A little way out of the village, on the side road by the telephone kiosk, there is a most interesting Iron Age Dun, or Fort. Unusually, it is a double construction, with one Dun enclosed within the walls of an earlier fortification. One wonders why this should be so.

If you have visited that Dun, and it is well worth a visit, then continue on the side road to its junction with A815 on the road south

to Loch Eck and Dunoon. About half a mile after Glenbranter
Bridge, off to the east, there are the grass covered foundations of
Driep House. Nothing else is left now, but three hundred years ago
Driep was a fine place, so fine that Mary, Queen of Scots, stayed
there in 1563. The Queen was making a grand progress through the
Highlands, and had landed from her Royal Ship at Creggans, by
Strachur.

Glenbranter was for many years the home of Sir Harry Lauder,
one of the best known Scots of all time. It was in Glenbranter House,
now demolished, that Harry Lauder, on New Year's Day in 1917,
learned of the death in France of his only son. Glenbranter never
again seemed the same, and shortly afterwards he left for good, but
did erect an obelisk to the memory of John Lauder. It stands on a
little knoll by the side of the road, looking out over the lovely glen.
There is also a Celtic Cross there, marking the place where Lady
Lauder was buried in 1927. But Sir Harry himself, although often
expressing the wish to lie in the same place, is buried far away in
Hamilton, with his own folk.

Loch Eck is a delight. Long and very narrow, it is also very
deep. The shores of Loch Eck, and all the hillsides, are tree-clad.

This is a fresh-water loch, of course, and with most excellent salmon and sea-trout fishing. On a bright, still day, the reflection of all the hills in Loch Eck is astonishing. It is difficult to determine which is hill and which reflection, and indeed the loch seems to disappear altogether.

Half way down the loch a grand side road climbs up onto the hills, through the forest, and runs down to Loch Long. It is a narrow and steep road, but eminently worth while, as it drops down through Glen Finart to Ardentinny on the shore of Loch Long. From there, a major road takes you quickly round Holy Loch to the fleshpots of Dunoon. And these could be very welcome after so many miles of travelling Highland roads and glorying in Highland scenery.

KILLER WHALES & GREY SEALS OFF ISLAY

-158-

DUNOON, COWAL, AND THE KYLES OF BUTE

Certainly this is the busiest part of Argyll and the most crowded with visitors. Of course the visitors crowd there because it is a lovely area and justly renowned for that. But the word 'crowd' is relative and certainly in this context it does not mean that you cannot find peace and solitude hereabouts.

As many visitors have discovered, there are some advantages in staying in or near a biggish town like Dunoon, enjoying the amenities that the town has, but also being very close to some extremely fine scenic delights. To begin with Dunoon.

Like some other towns up and down these lochs, Dunoon began to prosper with the railways and with fast steamers, when the wealthier citizens of Glasgow discovered that they could build their houses in such places, and yet still travel daily or weekly to their business in the sprawling and -- for them -- prosperous city. So Dunoon, like Helensburgh across the water, has many fine houses in excellent positions, and very many of them are today boarding houses and small hotels.

Of course, Dunoon is very close to Holy Loch, and that was, for many years, the centre in Britain of the American nuclear submarine fleet. Consequently Dunoon has undergone a sea-change, as young American service men and women mixed and mingled with the people of Dunoon and all the summer visitors -- with a certain confusion and puzzlement on both sides.

Now that the American base is closed, Dunoon will have to again find a new identity -- and that will not be easy after so many years of acting as host, and willing host at that, to so many and varied guests.

The Cowal Highland Gathering held in Dunoon each year must have been the most puzzling of all events for the trans-Atlantic transplants. Over a hundred pipe bands gather then, from all over the world, for two days of Highland fun and games. Pipers, dancers, tossers of the caber, throwers of the hammer, runners and exponents of every manner of Highland sport gather in their thousands for a test of skill, strength and sheer exuberance that is unparalleled. It is a wonderful and awesome sight to see the great mass of pipe bands parading through the streets of Dunoon.

Highland gatherings have come a long way since the days when the clansmen in remote glens practiced their skills and strength against each other in warlike games.

It might seem strange that the largest Highland gathering of all should take place in Dunoon, where there is hardly a shadow left of the old Highland language and Highland ways. Yet few places have had such a Highland history -- that is, death and pillage and blood shedding -- as this now pleasant town, and not two hundred years

ago, the only person to speak Lowland Scots or English in Dunoon
was the minister. The language of the people was Gaelic, but today
you are unlikely to hear a word of that ancient tongue.

Cowal -- the name derives from *Comgall*, one of the four
chiefs of the ancient kingdom of Dalriada -- has seen many invasions
from the days of the Mesolithic hunters and the Neolithic farmers,
and all left their traces and ruins for us to wonder at today.

This ancient history is perhaps most clearly seen at Ardnadam,
just outside Dunoon on the A885 road. This site could well have
been occupied as a domestic dwelling for over 4000 years. There are
Neolithic and Iron Age remains and a very early stone chapel. There
are the remains of every age up to about 1400 AD when iron
workers lived there. Remains of their charcoal burning can be seen in
the many round platforms cut into the hillside at this site.

Dunoon itself had a very ancient fort (*Dounare*, the old name
for Dunoon, tells us that), and in the 13th cent. must have had a

castle, for a Constable was appointed by the king as its commander. That would have been a Lamont castle, for the Lamonts were lords of Cowal long before the Campbells of Argyll were rooted there, for comparatively speaking the Campbells are upstarts.

The Lamonts had a second castle, south of Dunoon, at Toward, and between them those two castles saw such a scene of death and horror as even the Highlands can hardly parallel. The Campbells had taken Dunoon castle, and all of north Cowal during Robert Bruce's struggle for the Crown of Scotland, when the Lamonts, misguidedly, backed the weakling John Balliol. It was then that the '**Lord of Lochow (Campbell) and the Stewarts of Scotland landed in Cowall with their galleys and engines of war and besieged and took the castle of Dun Dounhone.**'

The Campbells always managed to keep what they had taken, and they kept Dunoon, and so there was ample cause for conflict with the Lamonts of Toward. It came to a head during the Civil War, on a summer day in 1646. Many old scores were settled during that Civil War: it was not just a conflict between King and Parliament, or Presbyterian and Episcopalian.

The Campbells attacked Toward, and the Lamonts capitulated. Then the terms of the capitulation were violated. The Campbells:-

'.....did most treacherously, perfidiously and traitorously fetter and bind the hands of near two hundred persons of the said Sir James' (Lamont) friends and followers, who were comprehended within the terms of the said capitulation, detaining them prisoners with a guard, their hands being bound behind their backs like thieves within the said Sir James' house and grounds of Toward, for the space of several days, in great torment and misery, and in pursuance of their further villainy, after plundering and robbing all that was within and about the same house, they most barbarously, inhumanly and cruelly murdered several young, old, yea, sucking children, some of them not one month old, and that the said persons, defendants, or one or others of them, contrary to the aforesaid capitulation, our laws and Acts of Parliament, upon the --- day of June 1646, most traitorously and perfidiously did carry the whole people who were in the said houses of Escog and Toward in boats to the village of Dunoon, and there most cruelly, traitorously and perfidiously, cause to hang upon one tree near the number of thirty six persons, most of them being special gentlemen of the name of Lamont, and vassals to the said Sir James....'**

Those who were not hanged were casually knifed.

But that was not the end of it. The Lamont men were hanged on a tree in the kirkyard of Dunoon. It was a 'lively, fresh-growing ash tree', but it was stricken dead in its prime, and when it was cut down two years later, out of its root there came a spring of blood, *'poppling up, running in several streams all over the roots'*, and this spring ran for several years until finally the roots of the tree were dug up by the murderers, because persons of all ranks resorted there to see it, and when the roots were dug up, all the ground was full of blood.

Make what you like of the ash tree and the blood, but the massacre certainly took place. There is a memorial to the dead Lamonts on top of the mound by Castle Hill in the middle of Dunoon, and that mound itself has a bloody history, for it was the moot hill where sentences were pronounced and justice (or punishments and retribution, rather) dispensed.

Dunoon Castle itself did not last long after the slaughter of the Lamonts. It was destroyed during Argyll's rebellion in 1685, when Atholl stormed down through Argyll, burning and killing.

Dunoon, of course, is one of the major gateways to the Highlands. The short ferry trip from Gourock, landing at Dunoon, is the quickest way into the Highlands from the south. And if, surprisingly, you don't want to spend time in Dunoon, then you can be out and away in ten minutes. But that would be a mistake, for Dunoon has plenty to make a visit there attractive. The grand promenade along the seafront is always pleasant, and the town has many little alleys and wynds that well repay exploration. Wander round by the castle hill, contemplate the monument to Highland Mary (the second love of Robert Burns's life), walk up Hillfoot Street (which, confusingly, is at the top of the hill), and enjoy the unspoiled atmosphere of the town.

The road south from Dunoon, past Toward castle, is very fine, and it takes you almost the full length of Loch Striven, which surely is one of the scenic delights of Scotland. There is no through road, so you must return the way you went, to Dunoon, but that return journey along Loch Striven will surely stay in your mind for ever.

Holy Loch is just north of Dunoon. There is a very fine Forestry Commission Arboretum by Kilmun on Holy Loch, with a fascinating display of exotic trees and shrubs. It is very much worthwhile walking there, up the hillside and looking away across the the Cowal hills. Avoid, if you can, looking at the loch. Near the arboretum is the ancient chapel of Kilmun, sacred to the memory of

St. Finton, who died in AD 635. It is more than possible that the strange name *Holy Loch* came from this chapel, although in fact there are several theories, none of them very convincing, about the origin of the name.

The burial place of the Campbells of Argyll is there at Kilmun, and there is the grave of the Earl Archibald, who was killed at Flodden. The establishment of this burial ground came about in a strange way, for this was Lamont country, not Campbell, and the two were not exactly compatible.

It happened that a young scion of the Campbells, Celestin, who was being educated in the Lowlands, died there in the depths of winter. His grief-stricken father, Duncan, the Black Knight, went to collect his son's body and carry it back to Loch Awe for burial. They were overtaken by a ferocious snow storm, and could force their way no further than Kilmun. They asked for help from Lamont, and he replied 'I, Great Lamont of all Cowal, do grant unto thee, Black Knight of Lochow, a grave of flags, wherin to bury thy son in thy distress.' The Black Knight was duly grateful, and endowed the church at Kilmun and later, in 1442, founded a college there, and with the agreement of Lamont, established the family burial ground we can still see.

It was David Napier, a remarkable, but now almost forgotten, Scots engineer who was largely responsible for the development and opening out of this area. In the middle years of last century, Napier was building steam ships, and fine ones. His vessels were plying up and down the Clyde, and into many of the Highland lochs. He was a first rate engineer, and made many developments and improvements to the machinery of the ships.

Napier saw no reason why, if steam was so successfully used to carry passengers and freight over the seas, it should not do the same over land, and so went ahead and designed steam-driven carriages or coaches. His vision was to establish roads through the Highlands on which his carriages could ply, and as a first step he bought land at Kilmun. He built a pier there, and houses, and an hotel, and soon Kilmun was an important staging post on the sea route between Glasgow and Inveraray. Then he built roads, and soon had his new-fangled steam carriages plying regularly from the pierhead. The idea was that passengers boarded a Napier steamer at the Broomielaw, in the heart of Glasgow, sailed to Kilmun, then took a steam carriage on to Loch Eck, where another Napier vessel carried them over the loch to met a second steam carriage taking them to Strachur, on Loch Fyne, where yet another vessel waited to take them on to Inveraray.

It was fine while it lasted, but the roads were rough, and the carriages not particularly reliable, and Napier, that fine pioneer of sea-going steam, was really too far in advance for his schemes of land travel to succeed. But it is a pity that he should virtually be forgotten, because he was a grand example of the self-taught, self-made Scottish entrepreneur.

A side road (not the B836, but the second, unclassified road) leads off A885 north of Dunoon at the head of Holy Loch. This leads some miles up into Glen Masson, and is very beautiful. Like so many others, this is a dead-end road. Before you reach the Glen Masson road, though, you pass the entrance to the Younger Botanical Garden, another of those delightful informal gardens which so enrich western Scotland. The collection of rhododendrons here is reputed to be the finest in the world, and if you can see them in May and June, in the glory of their flowering, you will not dispute that. The garden is not just rhododendrons, though. There are magnificent redwoods, and other conifers, and the whole garden, set in natural woodlands, is very fine. Go for the flowering if you can, but go anyway.

A very ancient manuscript, known as the Glen Masson MS, is in the National Library, Edinburgh. Its age is uncertain, but it contains *The Tale Of The Sons of Uisneach*, and it is that ancient manuscript which tells of the sorrows of Deirdre. That story is recounted in the section of this book dealing with Loch Etive, and placed firmly on the glorious shores of that loch. Frankly, there is rather more evidence that it all happened here, in Cowal, in the district now known as Glendaruel.

That manuscript gives us the lament of Deirdre, in which she sings of her love for the glens she has wandered with Naiose, and which they are to leave, she fears for ever, in order to return to Ireland.

> *Glen da Ruadh!*
> *Dear to me each of its native men,*
> *Sweet the cuckoo's note on bending bough*
> *On the peak above Glen da Ruadh.*

Whether Loch Etive or Loch Striven is not really important. Both well fit the tale: both are lovely enough to strain the very heart strings. And the tale has been told from time immemorial round the peat fires in Scotland and Ireland.

Glen Masson is wholly delightful at any time, but especially so when the river is in spate after rain. There is one place where the river plunges and roars over waterfalls and through cauldrons, fringed by hardwood trees and flower-decked banks. Here and there it has undercut the rocky river bed and left arches across the torrent. Quite beautiful.

Cowal is certainly not the easiest place to explore and enjoy by car. There are great tongues of land there, stretching southward into the Sound of Bute, and you can travel right round only one of them, the western one. For the others, you must be content with going so far round, to the end of the road, and then returning.

If you are coming from the north, by A815 through Strachur, you have a choice to make, for just by Strachur the road branches. The major road, A886, is new and fast, and gets you to the Kyles of Bute and Tighnabruich quickly. The old road hugs the shore of Loch Fyne, and has much to commend it.

Just south of the road junction on B8000, there is Castle Lachlan, and those old grey walls have seen some history. None of the history, perhaps, has been so romantic, and tragic, as that day in 1745 when MacLachlan decided to join his Prince, Charles Edward, who had raised his banner of revolt in far away Moidart. It was not easy for MacLachlan. He was not a great chief, and his land was surrounded by the land of the Campbells, who were naturally opposed to the Jacobite cause. He and his twenty men crossed Loch Fyne and landed at Crarae. As MacLachlan mounted his horse after the crossing, the restless horse turned three times against the sun, and this was very clearly an omen of evil.

The little band picked their way by hill tracks, and at night out of the Campbell country, and eventually to Edinburgh, where they joined the Prince with 180 men, MacLachlans and others they had picked up en route. They fought bravely and well, too, and the MacLachlans and the MacLeans fought on the right wing at Culloden. But bravery was not enough. MacLachlan and one of his sons were killed, and during the rebellion Toward castle was attacked and sacked, although later the MacLachlans had their lands restored to them. As well, perhaps, for they are one of the most ancient of Scottish families still in possession of hereditary lands, in their case going back to the 11th cent., and Castle Lachlan, under that name, was referred to during the reign of King Robert Bruce.

The road down the lochside is much quieter now than in the recent past, when it was the only road down to the Kyles of Bute. You can enjoy it now, and certainly it is not a road to hurry over. The loch and the hills are unfailingly delightful, and in every season present a tapestry of colour. Indeed, it is a road to linger over, and those who tarry most will see and enjoy most. It is not that there is anything of particular interest on the road; no tourist attractions of any kind intrude. It is just a succession of splendid views. Go, and enjoy it.

At Otter Ferry, coming south, you have a choice of roads. There used to be a ferry here, of course, over to Lochgilphead, but no more. By the way, don't expect to see otters at Otter Ferry, nor at the tiny village of Otter further south. The name is another corruption of the Gaelic, and comes from *Oitir* or sandy spit. At Otter Ferry you can turn eastward over the high and lonely road which joins the main A886 road at Clachan of Glendaruel. It is not the easiest choice

The Glendaruel Hotel

Clachan of Glendaruel
Argyll PA22 3AA

A small, friendly, fully-licensed country hotel, with a high level of comfort, amenities and good Scottish home cooking.

The *en suite* bedrooms have colour TV, tea/coffee makers, and central heating. There are two bars and a comfortable residents' lounge.

Our dining room offers an extensive *table d'hote* menu, including local fish, meat and game. We guarantee you will not go hungry, and are happy to prepare vegetarian or other diets.

There is fishing, stalking, hillwalking, golf, touring, and a wealth of bird and animal life all nearby, and you will find Glendaruel has a fascinating history.

Come and stay with us for an unforgettable holiday.

Tel: Glendaruel (036982) 274. Fax: (036982) 317.

to make. Personally, I always try to take that mountain road, at least to the summit at almost a thousand feet. And I will always stop and glory in the views -- Mull, Jura, Scarba, Corrievreckan and Lock Fyne are all there. See it at sunset, if you can. There will be the sound of wind sighing through the heather, the cry of a bird, the feel of soft Highland air or the ferocious sting of Highland rain, the smell of the land and of the sea. Truly an enchanted, even haunted, place, haunted by a history of battles and of faith and of loyalties and of deserted villages and fertile glens.

Glendaruel, incidentally, is yet another anglicised name distorted from the Gaelic on the maps, but this time it hides a subtle play on words. A battle was fought once by the bridge over the river Ruel. That was about 1110, when the Norsemen, commanded by the son of Magnus Barefoot, were met and defeated by the Scots. The dead Norsemen were thrown into the river, which had always been known as *Ruadh-thuil* -- Red Water -- because it was usually stained with peat. After the battle, the river became known as *Ruith-fhail*, or Bloody Water. The anglicised version loses this play on words so typical of the Gaelic language.

If you continue south from Otter Ferry the road turns inland, leaving the loch side and wandering through hills past Kilfinan, which was once the chief village in the district but is now a quiet and most attractive backwater. Kilfinan Bay, just off the road by the village, is a grand stretch of lovely sand, and well worthy of a day 'on the beach'. From Kilfinan it is south again to Millhouse, before turning north up to Tignabruich.

However, the last stretch of that road is by no means the best approach to Tighnabruich and the Kyles of Bute. If that is your destination, better to take the spectacular mountain road from Otter Ferry, and join the A886 at Clachan of Glendaruel. You then travel down the length of Loch Riddon, and are faced with a succession of views so delightful that every chocolate box should hide its head in shame. They are fine views, and no mistake, even though they do not have the grandeur which is the hallmark of the Highlands.

There is an excellent walk up Loch Riddon from near Tighnabruich. It follows the loch shore, with the road high above, and wanders charmingly through woods. You can look across the narrows to the Isle of Bute, and will surely see the Maids of Bute. These are two painted rocks, painted to resemble old women, and to most people it is a mystery how they got painted in the first place, since that corner of Bute is uninhabited. Even local people admit to puzzlement. As a matter of fact, the two rocks were first painted by Para Handy, skipper of the steam-puffer *Vital Spark* out of Glasgow, and how it happened is explained in the hilarious book about his voyagings.

It happened long before he rose to be skipper of the *Vital Spark*. He was a deck hand on the *Inverary Castle*, and the skipper of that vessel got quite angry when the English 'towerists' he occasionally carried could not see how those two rocks on Bute resembled two women, although the skippper, and Para Handy, insisted that they did. One day the skipper sent him ashore with tins of red and white paint to add clothes to the Maids, and before he had finished, Para Handy was half in love with both of them. Ever since, the paint has been renewed regularly, and Para Handy's first efforts improved out of all knowledge.

In many ways, the Kyles of Bute, with the Island of Bute across the narrow channel, are the prettiest part of Scotland. Naturally, there is no secret about this, and you must be prepared to share the beauty with many others. However, let there be no misunderstanding: it is not a spoiled beauty spot, spoiled by 'people pollution'. It is carefully preserved from that, and after all, you do not have to be there in the height of the holiday season.

The Kyles (another Gaelic word, meaning 'Narrow Water') run to the east and west of Bute itself, and nature has ordained that the views down both sides are very fine. But best of all, surely, are the views as one travels down the length of Loch Riddon. At all costs, travel south on that road: you will not be disappointed.

One of the problems of recommending places to go and things to see in Scotland is that whatever route one recommends, quite certainly something fine is omitted. I have taken you south from Strachur by the shores of Loch Fyne, and grand that certainly is. But if you take the main road south (A886) from Strachur, you have the chance of going through Glendaruel, and that is not something to be disregarded. Don't stay on the main road, though, unless you are in a particular hurry. Take the minor road to the left at Duror. It is a quiet backwater these days, and none the worse for that. It is a delightful glen, and if indeed this was where Deirdre and her lover spent their summer days, then they chose well.

LUATH PRESS

GUIDES TO SCOTLAND

SOUTH WEST SCOTLAND. Tom Atkinson. A guide book to the best of Kyle, Carrick, Galloway, Dumfries-shire, Kirkcudbrightshire and Wigtownshire. This lovely land of hills, moors and beaches is bounded by the Atlantic and the Solway. Steeped in history and legend, still unspoiled, it is not yet widely known. Yet it is a land whose peace and grandeur are at least comparable to the Highlands.

Legends, history and loving description by a local author make this an essential book for all who visit -- or live in -- the country of Robert Burns.

ISBN 0 946487 04 9. Paperback. £3:50p.

ROADS TO THE ISLES. Tom Atkinson. A guide book to Scotland's far north and west, including Ardnamurchan, Morvern, Morar, Moidart, and all the west coast to Ullapool.

This is the area lying to the west and north of Fort William. It is a land of still unspoiled loveliness, of mountain, loch and silver sands. It is a vast, quiet land of peace and grandeur. Legend, history and vivid description by an author who loves the area and knows it intimately make this a book essential to all who visit this Highland wonderland.

ISBN 0 946487 01 4. Paperback. £3:50p.

THE EMPTY LANDS. Tom Atkinson. A guide book to the north of Scotland, from Ullapool to Bettyhill, and from Bonar Bridge to John O' Groats.

This is the fourth book in the series, and it covers that vast empty quarter leading up to the north coast. These are the Highlands of myth and legend, a land of unsurpassed beauty, where sea and mountain mingle in majesty and grandeur. As in his other books, the author is not content to describe the scenery (which is really beyond description) or advise you where to go. He does all that with his usual skill and enthusiasm, but he also places that superb landscape into its historical context, and tells how it and the people who live there have become what we see today. With love and compassion, and some anger, he has written a book which should be read by everyone who visits or lives in -- or even dreams about -- that empty land.

ISBN 0 946487 13 8. Paperback. £3:50p.

HIGHWAYS AND BYWAYS IN MULL AND IONA.

Peter Macnab. In this newly revised guidebook to Mull and Iona, Peter Macnab takes the visitor on a guided tour of the two islands. Born and grown up on Mull, he has an unparalleled knowledge of the island, and a great love for it. There could be no better guide than him to those two accessible islands of the Inner Hebrides, and no-one more able to show visitors the true Mull and Iona.

ISBN 0 946487 16 2. Paperback. £3:25p.

Other books on the Scottish countryside

WALKS IN THE CAIRNGORMS. Ernest Cross. The
Cairngorms are the highest uplands in Britain, and walking there introduces you to sub-arctic scenery found nowhere else. This book provides a selection of walks in a splendid and magnificent countryside -- there are rare birds, animals and plants, geological curiosities, quiet woodland walks, unusual excursions in the mountains. Ernest Cross has written an excellent guidebook to those things. Not only does he have an intimate knowledge of what he describes, but he loves it all deeply, and this shows.

ISBN 0 946487 09 X. Paperback. £3:25p.

THE SPEYSIDE HOLIDAY GUIDE. Ernest Cross. Tooth-
ache in Tomintoul? Golf in Garmouth? Whatever your questions about Speyside, Ernest Cross has the answer in this Guide Book. Speyside is Scotland's ideal holiday centre. It has everything from the sub-arctic heights of the Cairngorms to the seemingly endless -- and quiet -- beaches. With a great wealth of peaceful towns and villages, it also possesses vast empty and open spaces, delightful to walk, a treasure to be discovered.

Ernest Cross knows and loves it all. In this book he directs you and guides you to the best of it. With his usual incisive wit and language, he introduces you to Scotland's most interesting area, and ensures that everyone, whether visitor or resident, is enriched by learning its secrets.

ISBN 0 946487 27 8. Paperback. £4:95p.

SHORT WALKS IN THE CAIRNGORMS. Ernest Cross.
A variety of shorter walks in the glorious scenery of the Cairngorms. It may be that you seek a stroll to the pub after dinner, or a half day on the high tops, or a guided two-hour walk round a loch. This book has them all, in profusion. You will be ably guided, and your guide will point out the most interesting sights and the best routes.

ISBN 0 946487 23 5. Paperback. £3:25p.

MOUNTAIN DAYS AND BOTHY NIGHTS. Dave Brown and Ian Mitchell. The authors have climbed, walked and bothied over much of Scotland for many years. There could be no better guide to the astonishing variety of bothies, howffs and dosses on the Scottish hills. They were part of the great explosion of climbing in the Fifties and Sixties, and they write of this with first-hand knowledge, sympathy and understanding.

Fishgut Mac, Desperate Dan, Stumpy and the Big Yin may not be on the hills any more, but the bothies and howffs they used are still there. There was the Royal Bothy, paid for by the Queen herself after an encounter with a gang of anarchist, republican hill-climbing desperadoes. There was the Secret Howff, built under the very noses of the disapproving laird and his gamekeepers. There was the Tarff Hotel, with its Three Star A.A. rating. These, and many more, feature in this book, together with tales of climbs and walks in the days of bendy boots and no artificial aids.

ISBN 0 946487 15 4. Paperback. £5:95p.

OTHER BOOKS FROM LUATH PRESS

TALES OF THE NORTH COAST. Alan Temperley and the pupils of Farr Secondary School. In this collection of 58 tales, there is a memorial to the great tradition of Highland story-telling. Simply told and unadorned, these tales are wide-ranging -- historical dramas, fairy tales, great battles, ship-wreck and ghosts, Highland rogues -- they all appear in this gallimaufry of tales, many of which have been told and re-told for generations round the fireside.

In addition to the tales, Alan Temperley has collected together a series of contemporary writings about the Clearances of Strathnaver, a central feature of local history, and a tragedy whose effects are still felt and discussed.

ISBN 0 946487 18 9 Paperback. £5:95.

POEMS TO BE READ ALOUD. *A Victorian Drawing Room Entertainment.* Selected and with an Introduction by Tom Atkinson. A very personal collection of poems specially selected for all those who believe that the world is full of people who long to hear you declaim such as these. The Entertainment ranges from an unusual and beautiful *Love Song* translated from the Sanskrit, to the drama of *The Shooting of Dan McGrew* and *The Green Eye of the Little Yellow God,* to the bathos of *Trees* and the outrageous bawdiness of *Eskimo Nell.* Altogether, a most unusual and amusing selection.

ISBN 0 946487 00 6. Paperback. £3:00p.

HIGHLAND BALLS AND VILLAGE HALLS. G.W.

Lockhart. There is no doubt about Wallace Lockhart's love of Scottish country dancing, nor of his profound knowledge of it. Reminiscence, anecdotes, social commentary and Scottish history, tartan and dress, prose and verse, the steps of the most important dances -- they are all brought together to remind, amuse and instruct the reader in all facets of Scottish country dancing. Wallace Lockhart practices what he preaches. He grew up in a house where the carpet was constantly being lifted for dancing, and the strains of country dance music have thrilled him in castle and village hall. He is the leader of the well known *Quern Players*, and he composed the dance *Eilidh MacIain*, which was the winning jig in the competition held by the Edinburgh Branch of the Royal Scottish Country Dance Society to commemorate its sixtieth anniversary.

This is a book for all who dance or who remember their dancing days. It is a book for all Scots.

ISBN 0 96487 12 X Paperback. £3:95p.

THE CROFTING YEARS. Francis Thompson. A remarkable

and moving study of crofting in the Highlands and Islands. It tells of the bloody conflicts a century ago when the crofters and their families faced all the forces of law and order, and demanded a legal status and security of tenure, and of how gunboats cruised the Western Isles in Government's classic answer. Life in the crofting townships is described with great insight and affection. Food, housing, healing and song are all dealt with. But the book is no nostalgic longing for the past. It looks to the future and argues that crofting must be carefully nurtured as a reservoir of potential strength for an uncertain future.

Frank Thompson lives and works in Stornoway. His life has been intimately bound up with the crofters, and he well knows of what he writes.

ISBN 0 946487 06 5. Paperback. £5:95p.

TALL TALES FROM AN ISLAND. Peter Macnab. These

tales come from the island of Mull, but they could just as well come from anywhere in the Highlands and Islands. Witches, ghosts, warlocks and fairies abound, as do stories of the people, their quiet humour and their abiding wit. A book to dip into, laugh over, and enthuse about. Out of this great range of stories a general picture emerges of an island people, stubborn and strong in adversity, but warm and co-operative and totally wedded to their island way of life. It is a clear picture of a microcosmic society perfectly adapted to an environment that, in spite of its great beauty, can be harsh and unforgiving.

Peter Macnab was born and grew up on Mull, and he knows and loves every inch of it. Not for him the 'superiority' of the incomer who makes joke cardboard figures of the island people and their ways. He presents a rounded account of Mull and its people.

ISBN 0 946487 07 3. Paperback. £6:50p.

BARE FEET AND TACKETY BOOTS. Archie Cameron.

The author is the last survivor who those who were born and reared on the island of Rhum in the days before the First World War, when the island was the private playground of a rich absentee landowner. Archie recalls all the pleasures and pains of those days. He writes of the remarkable characters, not least his own father, who worked the estate and guided the Gentry in their search for stags and fish. The Gentry have left ample records of their time on the island, but little is known of those who lived and worked there. Archie fills this gap. He recalls the pains and pleasures of his boyhood. Factors and Schoolmasters, midges and fish, deer and ducks and shepherds, the joys of poaching, the misery of MacBraynes' steamers -- they are all here.

This book is an important piece of social history, but, much more, it is a fascinating record of a way of life gone not so long ago, but already almost forgotten.

ISBN 0 946487 17 0. Paperback. £6:25p

ON THE TRAIL OF ROBERT SERVICE. G.W.

Lockhart. It is doubtful if any poet, except perhaps Robert Burns, has commanded such world-wide affection as Robert Service. It is doubtful if any verse has been recited more often than *The Shooting of Dan McGrew* and *The Cremation of Sam McGee.* Boy Scouts, learned Professors, armchair wanderers and active followers of the open road have all fallen under the spell of the man who chronicled the story of the Klondike Gold Rush. Too few know the story of the Scottish bank-clerk who became the Bard of the Yukon -- his early revolt against convention, his wandering vagabond years in the States and Canada, and his later travels in Tahiti and Russia.

This book tells the story of a man who captivated the imagination of generations, expressed the feelings and emotions of millions, and painlessly introduced countless numbers to the beauties of verse. Written with the full support of his family and containing some hitherto unpublished photographs, this book will delight Service lovers in both the Old World and the New.

ISBN 0 946487 24 3 Price: £5:95

THE BOTHY BREW. Hamish Brown. Hamish Brown is well known as a writer on Scottish, travel and outdoor subjects, as a photographer, lively lecturer, and editor of two poetry anthologies. His short stories have appeared in a wide range of publications.

He has climbed and travelled extensively in the Alps and less-known areas of Europe as well as in the remote Andes and Himalayas and each year spends some months in the south of Morocco. When not busy travelling and writing, home is at Kinghorn, with a view over the Forth to Edinburgh.

Although already the author of a dozen or so books, most of them reflecting his interest in and concern for the outdoors of Scotland, this is Hamish Brown's first collection of short stories.

This collection shows a remarkable range of interests and enthusiasms. They range from a murder on a beach at midnight to a family picnic at Loch Lomond, from a search for Painted Ladies in the mountains of Morocco to a search for a cuckoo in the Scottish hills.

These stories, although easy and a delight to read, yet show Hamish Brown's deep love for Scotland and the hills, and his profound knowledge of Scotland today.

ISBN 0 946 487 26 X. Paperback. Price: £5:95p.

COME DUNGEONS DARK. John Caldwell. The Life and Times of Guy Aldred, Glasgow Anarchist. Hardly a street-corner site in Glasgow did not know Guy Aldred's great resonant voice belabouring the evils of society. Hardly a Glasgow voter for three generations did not have the opportunity of electing him to the city or national government he despised so much, and vowed to enter only on his own terms if elected. But he never was elected, although he once stood simultaneously for fourteen city wards. He claimed there was better company in Barlinnie Prison (which he knew well) than in the Corridors of Power.

Guy Alfred Aldred was born on November 5th 1886, and died on 16th October 1963. He had just 10 pence in his pocket when he died. Boy-preacher, Social Democrat, Prisoner of Conscience, Conscientious Objector, Anarcho-Communist, orator, writer, publisher -- Guy Aldred never ceased struggling for those things in which he believed. He was part of Glasgow's history, and must never be forgotten.
ISBN 0 946487 19 7. Paperback. Price £6:95p.

SEVEN STEPS IN THE DARK. Bob Smith. The life and times of a Scottish miner. Before it is too late, before the last Scottish miner has hung up his lamp for the last time, Bob Smith has recorded his lifetime's work in the mines of Scotland. He started work in the pit when he was fourteen, working with his father, when every ton of coal was cut by hand with a pick, when ponies dragged it to the shaft, and every penny of pay was fought for against a grasping coal-owner.

He saw his industry nationalised, then mechanised, and finally destroyed. He worked in the pits for forty years, until injury forced his retirement. He was an active Tades Unionist all his life, and a Lodge Official for many years. He experienced strikes, and was always at the sharp end of the struggle for safety and better conditions. This is a miner's view of history, and records the reality behind the statistics and the rhetoric of politicians and managers and Trades Union officials.

ISBN   0 946487 21 9   Price: £8:95p.

REVOLTING SCOTLAND. Jeff Fallow

A book of cartoons, showing Scotland of yesterday and today.
GREETINGS FRAE BONNY SCOTLAND!
Yes, but which Scotland?
Definitely not the Scotland of Heilan' Flings, Porridge and Haggis.
Certainly not the Scotland of Kilty Dolls, Mean Jocks and Tartan Trivia.
This is Scotland as it is, and Scotland as it was, and Scotland as it will be.
It is a book of cartoons, some very funny, some very bitter, and all very true.
You might learn more about Scottish history from these cartoons than you ever did at school.
If you are a visitor, you will understand more. If you are a Scot, you might just feel like getting up and doing something about it.

ISBN 0946487 23 1. Paperback. 130 pages. Price £5:95p.

Any of these books can be obtained from your bookseller, or, in case of difficulty, please send price shown, plus £1 for post and packing, to:
LUATH PRESS LTD.

BARR, AYRSHIRE. KA26 9TN

Tel: Barr (046-586) 636